Shamanism for Beginners

Explore Shamanic Rituals, Beliefs, and Practices of Native American, Norse, Celtic, and Siberian Shamans

Free Bonus from Silvia Hill available for limited time

Hi Spirituality Lovers!

My name is Silvia Hill, and first off, I want to THANK YOU for reading my book.

Now you have a chance to join my exclusive spirituality email list so you can get the ebooks below for free as well as the potential to get more spirituality ebooks for free! Simply click the link below to join.

P.S. Remember that it's 100% free to join the list.

~~$27~~ FREE BONUSES

- 🙌 9 Types of Spirit Guides and How to Connect to Them
- 🙌 How to Develop Your Intuition: 7 Secrets for Psychic Development and Tarot Reading
- 🙌 Tarot Reading Secrets for Love, Career, and General Messages

Access your free bonuses here

https://livetolearn.lpages.co/shamanism-for-beginners-paperback/

Table of Contents

Introduction

Since humanity first crawled from the oceans, heaving itself onto dry land, we have yearned for union with something just on the fringes of our material existence. Instinctively, we reached toward what was not quite beyond our experience but was somehow adjacent to it. We knew it was there and intimately related to the life of matter. We knew that whatever the mysterious adjacent truth was, it was part of us, and we were part of it.

Shamanism is widely understood to be an early manifestation of our human desire to get closer to whatever that adjacent, unseen world means. The word "shaman" is derived from the Russian word "šamán," and according to the Golomt Center for Shamanic Studies located in Mongolia, it is usually translated to mean priest.

Rooted in humanity's earliest observations of the natural world and our place in it, Shamanism's overarching model is community. While that model is shared by most (if not all) religious systems we can name, only Shamanism's model includes Creation itself as a member of the community. In the traditional practice of Shamanism, there is no division between the human being, other animals, the elements of Creation, and Creation itself. It is all one community, and the Shaman's place in that community is that of *Healer*.

Growing from Creation itself (as an appointed spiritual healer and intentional spiritual traveler of the cosmos), the Shaman embodies the values of Creation: goodness, nurture, and unconditional love. While that may sound like an anthropomorphized view of the environmental systems and energies comprising Creation, early humanity operated from the unique perspective of its time, just as we do. That perspective has much to offer the humanity of the 21st Century.

In "Shamanism for Beginners," we will visit shamanic cultures worldwide and discuss the vast global tradition of Shamanism, humanity's oldest and most enduring form of worship and spiritual exploration. We will explore the themes and practices common to most Shamanic cultures and how they can help us heal the ills of our world while honoring their traditions and primacy as vehicles of spiritual knowledge.

As stated above, humans of the 21st Century can learn much from our ancestors. United in an ancient common experience of Shamanic practices and beliefs, we have so much more in common than we think. Let's reconnect with the ground beneath our feet and discover the riches of a life lived in spiritual humility, in community with the Creation we form part of.

Chapter One: The Wounded Healer

No living human gets off the planet alive. Human life is a weird rollercoaster ride, falling and rising and falling again, twisting, turning, then finally arriving at its unseen destination with a screech, when least expected.

The Shaman.

As we ride the rollercoaster of life, we get a lot of dings, bumps, and scrapes. Scars bear witness to our fragility. Surgery, illness, and accidents take their toll as we move from death-defying curve to stomach-contracting plummet with a faint shriek of alarm. But only some are called to be the Wounded Healer.

Socrates once wrote that "*Madness* is a divine gift." Nowhere is this more evident than in the vocation of a Shaman, which requires the presence of a profound wound. Through that wound, the Shaman penetrates the depths of this cosmos, emerging with an answer to that suffering not of the individual alone but including all that is.

This concept that suffering is a teacher is also present in modern monotheistic religions. Roman Catholicism draws heavily on it but as a means of offering a theodicy, a rationale for why bad things happen to good people. In that Western framework, suffering is primarily explained as a means by which a distant (yet ever near and implicated) Creator bestows wisdom upon us. The intention is to lighten the load represented by suffering. The question is answered by explaining why suffering is permitted to plague children of a loving God instead of merely being contemplated. True meaning is lost, and an overarching panacea is applied.

In Shamanism, suffering's purpose is to break open the spiritual heart, releasing from it the knowledge of all suffering in all ages. Suffering is the legacy of both the living and the dead, and in the world of the Shaman, there is only a veil between the two, allowing the Shaman, through the practices associated with Shamanism of various kinds, to breach that veil. By doing so, the Shaman is empowered to gather the wisdom of all human life, returning to the material world with loving assistance, courtesy of the ancestors.

The Wounded Healer

Socrates' "madness as a divine gift" is fully realized in the Shamanic tradition, where the Shaman's wound is the defining feature of the community's appointed cosmonaut. Through that wound, the Shaman passes from this world into that of the spirits, with a foot in both worlds. A mediating force, the Shaman, draws from the wound of madness, death, illness, or tragedy the divine truth it conceals. In that singular power is the foundation of one who speaks for the fundamental integrity of all that is, living, dead, material, and ethereal.

Beyond the wound, there are several hallmarks sought out in Shamans in most if not all traditional Shamanic societies. You may see something of yourself in what follows.

At-One-Ment

The Shaman has a natural understanding of the interconnected nature of material reality. This understanding comes as naturally to the Shaman as the understanding that the spirit world is not only real but an intimate part of what it means to be human. This holistic worldview is best described as *"at-one-ment."*

The word "atonement" describes the intention to compensate for wrongs committed with penitence as compensation for the injury occasioned by one's actions. But when the word is approached differently and broken down into its syllables, we arrive at an entirely different meaning. Atonement is intended to bring the sinner/wrongdoer into communion with God and the community. In the same way, the Shaman naturally understands atonement as *at-one-ment*, cutting to the chase. Because in Shamanism, healing is the thing. What is described as penitence in all three Monotheistic Faiths, Judaism, Christianity, and Islam, becomes reconciliation in Shamanism. Without prescriptions about what constitutes "sin," wrongdoing, or injury, Shamanism is a bearer of healing, imparted to all Creation in the individual, the community, and the Creation they exist in.

At-one-ment is healing. It is the closing of the wound. While the wound of the Shaman remains open, the wounds of others are closed. The Shaman's wound acts as a portal through which the energies that constitute all Creation may move freely, unimpeded. This portal is the key to at-one-ment, for it dwells in the Shaman as the truth about humanity and its place in the greater order of things.

At-one-ment is experienced in many ways, but the Shaman's inclination to the natural world, its wild places, and its living things is the locus of the Shaman's awakening to the adjacent world, which speaks through nature itself. In the whispers of leaves moving in the wind, in the soft give of moss under a human foot, the adjacent, spiritual world breathes softly, speaking to the Wounded Healer. And so, in nature, the Shaman is awakened and called.

The Joy of Isolation

A Shaman is not a social butterfly. Rather, the Wounded Healer prefers silence, tranquility, and the joy of isolation. In traditional Shamanic societies, the Shaman dwells at a distance, set apart as a holy person.

Shamans of all traditions are known as introspective people whose wounded status confers spiritual gifts that require nurture. Most modern societies aren't that hospitable to those inclined toward Shamanism. Introversion and introspection are frowned upon by most people, making the quiet person who keeps themselves to themselves a suspect for any number of perceived social faux pas.

The world's noise drowns out the quiet wisdom of the Shaman, and so, the Shaman is one given to retreating to the calm of quiet reflection and communion with the truth of cosmic unity.

Mysticism in Suffering

"I will soothe you and heal you. I will bring you roses. I, too, have been covered with thorns." Rumi

The Wounded Healer has survived an experience of resurrection. This is not a literal resurrection in the manner of Jesus of Nazareth. This is a spiritual resurrection provoked by a catastrophe. Profound illness, surviving a disaster or war, or any other extreme event can be the source of a mystical experience that points the wounded person toward shamanic vocation.

Suppose you have undergone serious surgery, been in a car accident, or survived armed conflict. In that case, you will know that experiences of such an extreme nature impact us in mysterious ways. We may be physically injured or altered, permanently or temporarily disabled, and we *may go mad.* But in the wound is the gift. The mystery guides the sufferer to the heart of the cosmos within the madness, the injury, the mayhem, and the horror.

Waking up to your own vulnerability and woundedness is an awakening to the truth. Not everyone dares to do it, but the Shaman embraces the journey of the wound's full flowering as union with all that is.

Seeing Past the Surface

Most of us move through life blissfully ignorant of the energies all around us, particularly those of other people. We take people at face value. We believe what they say. We project our "niceness" onto them, mistaking everyone for someone with intentions as pure as our own.

But the Shaman sees past the surface. The gaze of the Wounded Healer penetrates to the core. There is no escape from the knowing regard of one who can discern the truth about people, their foibles, and their casual mendacity. Shamans can read people like books.

As you wear your worldly mask, the Shaman's gaze detects the truth you hide behind it, the wounds you conceal with a smile. Your spiritual condition is laid bare under the eyes of the Wounded Healer, connected to a reality that encompasses us all.

The Gift of Prophecy

Dreams come to us for many reasons. They may resolve the events of the day, recall past trauma, or unveil sources of anxiety. But there are also dreams which reveal information about events that haven't yet come to pass.

Prophetic dreams come to those whose spirits are connected to the adjacent world we mentioned earlier. These dreamers have ready access to the spirit world and knowledge of the souls who reside there. Prophetic dreams cannot be induced. They simply occur. We may not understand them at first, but, in prayerful reflection, we can interpret their meaning.

The Wound Healer's dreams bear whispers of the future, wrapped in complex signs and symbols, revealing the way forward.

Animals (or Hybrids)

The Shaman's openness and adaptability to the fullness of reality (encompassing the spirit world) means visits from spirit animals or human/other species hybrids, for example, the Minotaur-half bull, half human. These visitors bear messages from the adjacent world.

The spirit animal will be discussed later in this book when we meet some of the more likely suspects and learn about what they mean.

A Fire in the Belly

The fire in a Wounded Healer's belly is the fire of love. That love represents vocation. When the impulse is toward helping others in the massive project of healing the wound's creation, there is potential for Shamanic vocation.

Love is the greatest prerequisite for a Shaman. But that love is active, healing, and holy. We're not talking about "thoughts and prayers," we're talking about a love that makes a difference by acting. "Orthopraxy" literally means "right action" or pursuing the promptings of spirit by acting according to those promptings. This is the Shaman's work in a nutshell.

As you move through this book, you will be exploring traditional Shamanism. Specifically, the book talks about the practices of First Nations (Native populations of the Americas), Norse, Celtic, and Siberian shamanic cultures. It will also discuss neo-Paganism and the contemporary iteration of Shamanism.

What is important to remember, and something that should be addressed at this early stage of your journey, is that traditional practices are not for everyone. They are not to be trifled with, abused, or misappropriated. That doesn't imply that Shamanism may not be practiced by anyone outside the cultures from which it springs. Just be aware that you are practicing something ancient and established, something that is part of cultures of which you're most likely not a member. Having respect for the traditions of others is the first work of a Shaman because the integrity of life on this fragile earth goes sideways when respect is lacking.

The Shaman heals. The Shaman does not hurt, so tread lightly and with awe when approaching Shamanism, humanity's oldest form of worship. If you're reading out of interest or because you believe you have a Shamanic vocation, these ancient ways are the ways of all humanity - or once were. We all have some knowledge of these ways, or we wouldn't understand the concept of community or the importance of healing for the resolution of trauma. We know that humans live most successfully in communities. We know that trauma is the root of so much evil and suffering in this world. We know that healing trauma heals communities, and humans get closer to healing Creation in healing communities.

We know all these things, but we have lost the thread. Having elevated individualism to a major cultural value, the West has become a fractured landscape in which many are expendable for the benefit of a few. Shamanism stands as the human way of existing in today's world, maintaining the integrity of the whole for the good of everyone. When one is broken, the precious web of life is breached, and we all become vulnerable. Creation becomes vulnerable. We can see this is true simply by observing the massive changes in the global climate, the pandemic, the rise of totalitarianism, and unrest worldwide.

The Wounded Healer is charged with caring for one small corner of the larger community. A network of Wounded Healers is needed, from all cultures and every corner of the world, to affect the healing of Creation in the microcosm, the community for which the Shaman stands as the conduit for healing spiritual power.

In the next chapter, we'll explore the beliefs and cosmologies of Shamanism from First Nations, Norse, Celtic, and Siberian traditional cultures. You'll be fascinated by the connections between them, forged in times when the only possible communicative connection between disparate peoples was that of spirit.

Chapter Two: Traditional Beliefs and Cosmologies

At the very heart of Shamanism is animism. Widely misunderstood as a belief in animal gods, animism is, in truth, what we understand as "pantheism," the belief that all is animated by an ethereal spirit/soul, even those elements of Creation we consider "inanimate."

Pantheism differs only semantically from animism. Animism posits a unique spirit in all things, while pantheism posits a universal spirit that animates every being or thing (with the spirit of whichever god is under discussion). Theologically speaking, this position could be argued as vigorously as the Scholastics of the Christian Church once debated the number of angels capable of dancing on the head of a pin. But clearly, the idea of an individual, eternal spirit is the basis of Shamanism. Pantheism, on the other hand, attributes the animation of all things to the spirit of one god (by whatever name) – god in all. But in Shamanism, there is usually no god seen as a benevolent, ordering spirit overall. There is Creation and its inhabitants, united as a single reality as individual strands in the web of Creation, with humans as curator-participants. The Scholastic argument may well be had, but it has little momentum.

The most ancient expression of human spirituality was not codified or evangelized. It was received as a gift of spiritual instinct and observation by humans. No council was held in an ancient city, no submission to the will of a distant God. There was only life and what it taught our ancestors about how the world was or was then. Humans created Shamanism in disparate parts of the world, in widely varying cultures, without virtue of direction from a House of Bishops, Rabbis, or Mullahs. Humans looked around them and sought answers from the ground beneath their feet, the sky over their heads, the stones, the mountains, the rivers, and the seas. Our souls once lived in union with our earthly home because we knew who we were and what was required of us.

Cosmology – The Big Questions

It is always helpful to define terms, so let's start with this one. Cosmology defines what we think about where we came from, why we are here, and our role in Creation. The Judeo-Christian-Muslim cosmology involves the Creation of all that is by the hand of the Divine Creator.

Simply put, scientific cosmology suggests a cataclysmic explosion, resulting in life as we know it. Said life then develops (evolution) into its eventual form. But where does that development end? Sadly, it doesn't seem that evolution has concluded, with wisdom teeth being the most compelling evidence to that effect! Who needs 'em, right?

So, the cosmologies we're most familiar with within our society are those of the major monotheistic Faiths and that of science. But what does a cosmology of experience, both spiritual and physical, mean? How does it challenge those more familiar cosmologies? Let's explore the question through the lens of Shamanism and the cultures that continue to practice it.

First Nations

The First Nations of the Americas (North, Central, and South) are the most vibrant living examples of Shamanistic cultures in existence. Formed of various tribes with varying traditions, Shamanism is a common thread running through them all, just as it is in all aboriginal communities worldwide. What changed most human cultures was the advent of colonialism.

First Nations, due to their location in the resource-rich Americas, were some of colonialism's most abused victims. Africa, Polynesia, and other colonized cultures suffered similarly. No one escaped the imposition of the colonial Faith. But as time passed, recovery occurred.

Today, the living cultures of First Nations across the Americas are being revived, with traditional beliefs and languages resurrected from colonialism's ashes. This painful but invigorating process now has the support of governments in Canada, the United States, Mexico, and many others. Now taking their seat at the table against great odds and furious opposition, First Nations people are restoring their ways by demanding them.

Importantly, First Nations' tribal entities have distinct creation stories, varying wildly. But at the core of each, nature takes the lead, bestowing humanity a special role. Let's examine two such narratives.

Apache (USA)

The Apache people have many versions of how everything and everyone got here, but one of the more popular ones involves a wizened old man with a beard, described as "One Who Lives Beyond." As Creation "wakes up," this little old man begins to rub his hands and face, bringing the elements to life.

Once created, all these elements (or gods, if you will) shook hands. The little old man then directed the elements to drag a ball he had deliberately dropped in a circle, creating the boundaries of the Earth. A hummingbird then guided the One Who Lives Beyond to establish the four directions, stabilizing the new Earth. Key to this narrative for our purposes is the implication of an animal helper and the human form which was taken by the One Who Lives Beyond.

Haida (Canada)

The Pacific Coast of Canada is home to several First Nations cultures holding a creation story in which a raven is the creator. While the raven is a feature of many First Nations cultures in the region (the Pacific Southwest of Canada), the raven creation story is most vibrantly understood and cleaved to by the Haida people.

The world was completely dark, and the raven found that he was bumping into things, so he resolved to bring light. As he stumbled around on his quest, the raven came upon an old man who lived with his daughter. In conversation, the raven discovered that the old man had the most amazing and valuable treasure concealed in a small box. This was the light the raven sought to bring to the world, so he resolved to rob the old man.

The Raven became a pine needle, dropping into the river as the old man's daughter gathered it. Drinking the water, she became pregnant, giving birth to the raven in human form. As a baby, the raven won the old man's heart. The raven leveraged this affection to get at the light in the box. When the old man finally consented to show him the light, the raven's form was restored, and as the old man threw the glowing light to the now massive, dark bird, the raven caught it and flew away, taking the light out into the world.

Again, we see a human agency working in tandem with the spirit world, but in the Haida narrative, the raven tricks the human into relinquishing a gift intended for all of Creation. And so, the sneakiness of the raven is redeemed by the vastness of the eventual gift, even if the raven was originally only tired of stubbing his claws in the dark.

The common feature of humanity working with nature is flipped on its head in the Haida Creation narrative, with the raven demanding of humanity a public resource that shouldn't be stored in a box. Even through deception, the raven provided necessary help to Creation, and humanity was robbed of its impulse to privatization by the raven's action.

These are only two examples of the vast storehouse of First Nations' creation narratives extent in the Americas. As we have seen, some peoples have more than one narrative. Not written in stone, the First Nations creation narrative is rooted in natural phenomena. As we have seen, birds figure prominently, but other creatures also appear. The interplay in the narrative is always between two creatures, communicating freely in the spiritual world of creation, a coming to materiality, and the first of many communal projects shared by creatures in Creation.

Norse

The ancient Norse Shamanic tradition is somewhat familiar, as most readers will know about Thor and his infamous hammer. Interesting to note is that Norse Shamanism is the last of the European traditions to have succumbed to the march of Christianity. But the Norse cosmology is quite unique among Shamanic cultures and, thus, worthy of mention.

The cosmology of the Norse Shamanic tradition is that of nine distinct worlds with a tree holding them together (see Chapter 8). Norse Shamanism also features a distinct pantheon, with Odin as the chief deity. Odin, however, is very similar in most instances to Thor, with the two sharing attributes and roles. But there are also distinct differences between these two figures in Norse Shamanism. For one, Thor is subordinate to Odin. Odin is at the top of the cosmological hierarchy. While Thor is associated with thunderbolts and, of course, that hammer, Odin is associated with wisdom, often depicted as a traveler of a lowly estate. Further, Thor is the impetuous son of Odin, the wise "top god" of the Norse pantheon.

Norse Shamanism is known as "forn sidr," or the "old way," referring to its ancient origins. The cosmology and beliefs of the old way are mostly unknown due to the oral transmission of these traditions. Today, vestiges of Norse Shamanism can be found in revivalist tendencies like native Paganism, rooted in ancient Norse Shamanism. The origins of the old way are largely lost to time, but it is believed they stemmed from still more ancient examples of animism and other pre-existing forms of Shamanism.

Shared with the Ancient Romans is the belief in an afterlife, expressed as "Valhalla," the hall of those slain in battle, to be in the presence of Odin. Half of the slain in battle were transported to Valhalla by the famed Valkyries, while the other half was taken by the goddess Freyja to Folkvangr, a field in the afterlife for those slain in battle. In that field was Freyja's own hall, Sessrumnir, where, as they do in Valhalla, the slain chowed down on fine food and drank beer.

Norse Shamanism may no longer be said to exist in any tangible way. Followers rely on sparse information to reconstruct the old way, resulting in modern iterations called Odinism,

Heathenry, and Germanic Neo-Paganism. There are estimated to be about 20,000 people following a version of the old way, mostly residing in Scandinavian countries.

An unfortunate truth about Norse Shamanism (closely related to Germanic Shamanism, see above) is the misappropriation of the old way by the Third Reich. Deploying symbols and motifs from the ancient religion, the Nazis created an ideology supported by the assertion that the old way demanded "racial purity." An example, the Othala rune, is shown below. Neo-Nazi groups regularly employ this rune to get around the familiarity and associations of the Swastika with genocide, but the image below makes it clear that those associations continue to be active within the symbol.

The Othala rune.

User:Marco Kaiser, CC BY-SA 4.0 <https://creativecommons.org/licenses/by-sa/4.0>, via Wikimedia Commons: https://commons.wikimedia.org/wiki/File:Odal,_Othala_Rune_SS.png

Ironically symbolizing "life," the Othala rune was enthusiastically deployed by the Third Reich in connection with its assertions about "racial" purity and the importance of protecting it. (If you would like to see more misappropriated Norse shamanic symbols deployed today by both Neo-Nazis and white supremacists, please visit the link in the Resources section.) This note is added not to smear the old way but rather to warn that the symbols associated with Norse Shamanism have been compromised by their continuing misuse in the hands of corrosive ideologies, something you should be aware of.

Celtic

Described by adherents as "seership," Celtic Shamanism, like its Norse cousin, has been subject to the fantasies of post-modernism and its almost psychotic drive to appropriate things which don't belong to it. There is an ancient foundation in play that must not be disrespected by inaccuracies born in the minds of people desperately seeking meaning. Meaning must be sought in truth, not fantasies.

In about 1500 BCE, the Celts migrated from what is believed to be Asia Minor to Eastern Europe and in and around Germany, later colonizing the islands now called Great Britain. A large Celtic community settled in the Danube basin of Hungary, most likely on the way north, having found what they wanted in this fertile, abundant area. They brought with them, wherever they settled, the distinct "old way" of Shamanism.

And the word "Shamanism" is somewhat misleading with respect to Celtic Shamanism, as the role of the Shaman was realized by more than one person appointed to safeguard and maintain the spiritual health of the community.

The ban feasa (woman of knowledge) and the ban leighis (woman of healing) were responsible for dispensing remedies and rituals for healing. Both women could break spells cast on their patients and cast out demonic presences.

In Celtic Shamanism, keeping in mind the naming of the tradition as "seership" by followers, the work of the oracle is exceptionally strong. Seers, in Celtic Shamanism, were charged with seeking signs and omens to vet the intentions of communal actions and their wisdom and bring healing actions to the community. Finally, there were the ban chaointe or "keeners." These were the women who sent the departed to the world of the spirits.

This brings us to the role of "psychopomp" in Shamanism and its importance to the overall constructs of nature-based faith systems emanating from the Ancient World. Like the other roles fulfilling the work of the Shaman in this iteration of Shamanism, the psychopomp was connected to the spirit world, able to move between it and the material world without impediment. The keeners were themselves psychopomps, conducting the souls of those leaving this world to their new home with the aid of specific sounds and actions, infused with the energy of emotion and spiritual mastery. But the psychopomp of ancient times and in many shamanic traditions was an animal, like Anubis, appointed to conduct the dead across the river Styx and into the underworld. The psychopomp did not judge. The psychopomp did a necessary job, which was to affect the transition of human souls from this life to the next.

Woman-centered and deeply connected to nature, the core cosmology of Celtic Shamanism was simple and animistic. There was no pantheon. There was humanity acting in harmony and in concert with the natural world through observation of signs and symbols, helping them interpret their lives and events occurring in them. Not unlike the First Nations' shamanic traditions, which thanked animals for becoming food, Aal of nature was praised in this tradition (from the cow that provided milk to the earth that provided soil to grow fruit, roots, and vegetables.

The Oran Mor was the great Celtic hymn. Its name is translated as the "Great Melody" or the "Never-Ending Song." In the Celtic shamanic tradition, this song was meant to represent the breath of God at Creation, sweeping over the waters of chaos. But the breath of God doesn't end once Creation is accomplished, and so, the Great Melody continues, ever sighing over a Creation that lives, grows, breathes, and nurtures every moment. Because this hymn was central to Celtic Shamanism, it is reproduced here:

The Oran Mor

Quiet. Eternal quiet.
"Not even the sound of the restless, stirring dark waters could be heard. Then, a great, spiraling strain of melody moved across the endless waters.
Subdued at first, then quickly gathered momentum until it reached a great crescendo.
And then, there was life!
But the melody did not stop.
It continued its song,
Filling all Creation with its divine harmony.
And so, it continues today
For all those who will listen. "

Some will say that the Oran Mor sounds suspiciously like the Creation story in Genesis. It is worth submitting that it is the other way around!

Siberian

While some consider Siberia to have been the kernel from which all other shamanic societies grew, there is no question that of all the shamanic belief systems we have reviewed in this chapter, only First Nations' and Siberian Shamanism continue to be widely practiced in forms that are either close to their original traditions or the same. The other forms of Shamanism enumerated can't say that. Modern iterations of these traditions tend to be syncretic, cobbling together clues to form the basis of revival. This delegitimizes no one's practice. It is simply the reality of reviving ancient traditions that have lain dormant for long periods. The lack of codification (books) is the reason for this. When oral transmission ceases, usually because a colonizing religious force has inserted itself into the culture's territory, so do the original traditions. Only those observations written after the fact, based on archaeology and anthropology, remain to guide modern followers, naturally resulting in the original form emerging as a shadow of its former self.

With Siberia as the epicenter, North Asia is the home to various ethnic peoples practicing Shamanism. Their belief is that Siberia is the Shaman of all Shamans and the original upon which all others are based. Siberian Shamanism posits that Siberia is a spirit/Shaman which shared shamanic knowledge only with certain people, rendering them able to act as intermediaries between the material world and that of the spirits. The legend goes that the peoples of Siberia shared their sacred knowledge, which dispersed to the far reaches of the Earth, sharing shamanic knowledge with the world and, in so doing, saving people. This is at the heart of Siberian Shamanism; that Shamanism is, in its practice, salvific.

The integrity of Siberian Shamanism is why researchers continue to assert its primacy as the possible origin of all shamanisms. And this is entirely possible but unimportant. What is important is that this cultural tradition stands out as unique in a world (especially in the European or Eurasian world) that has largely moved on from Shamanism as a belief system in favor of the major monotheistic faiths.

Commonalities

Common to all world shamanisms is the connection to nature. While martial systems like Norse Shamanism and the Buryat practices (which uplift the value of the warrior and the defense of territory), most Shamanism has little interest in such pursuits. For the most part, shamanic societies are dedicated to a gentler way of living on the Earth they know they are not just an integral part of but are at one with.

Except in the Norse iteration, animism is the primary position of Shamanism, with the belief that all is animated by a spirit being central. But 5 core beliefs stand as common to all shamanic belief systems:

1. Healing. Shamans do not choose to be who they are. They are called

2. Shamans can deftly transit between the material and spirit worlds (called ordinary and non-ordinary reality)

3. Shamans can alter their state of consciousness to enter non-ordinary reality on behalf of the community

4. Physical objects are used to extract healing energies for patients in the community

5. The role of the Shaman is to heal and, by so doing, to fulfill his or her responsibility to the people being spiritually served. The Shaman's work is a celebration of life's holiness and humanity's holy mission

This chapter is a basic overview of 4 key shamanic world traditions. Please keep in mind that we are discussing the ancient traditions in this chapter, not the modern iterations of them. You are therefore encouraged to avail yourself of the Resources section at the conclusion of this book to gain a deeper understanding.

In the next chapter, you will discover some of the tools used by Shamans in the course of their work and how they are used.

Chapter Three: Shamanic Tools and Instruments

Technology is an amazing field of human endeavor which has both liberated and enslaved us. On the one hand, we can reach out to people across the world with technology facilitated by various communication systems and devices. We can fly to the moon and get up close and personal with other planets in our solar system. On the other hand, we are addicted to the use of technology, and our mobile devices have become almost integral to our lives – and our bodies. Tell me your phone isn't constantly cradled in your hand, stuck in your pocket, or ready for action on your nightstand. God forbid you should miss a text, a call, or the latest phantasmagorical breaking news item.

Technology is a double-edged sword, and nowhere is that truer than in the spiritual world. Shamanism hasn't been an exception to the proliferation of technological supports deployed in worshipping faith communities. Megachurches are hotbeds of technology, featuring big screens and state-of-the-art sound systems, among many other bells and whistles. The discussion in this chapter is a perfect example of technological creep.

Sound is a key element of the practice of shamanic journeying. Shamans traditionally used drums and rattles to create a soundscape conducive to achieving a trance state. But today, modern Shamans increasingly rely on binaural beats to enter this state of consciousness. Not that there is anything wrong with that.

But from the Luddite perspective, the visceral immediacy of naturally produced sound has far greater power in the context of spirituality. While binaural beats may provide a technological substitute that offers convenience in certain circumstances, anyone who has ever heard percussion instruments played live knows that nothing can replace the thunder of the drums as they reverberate through your body to the core of your being. That sensation has a familiarity to it. We have heard or felt it before, through our ancestors. The drums have always been part of our lives, filling them with a nurturing heartbeat, so we respond to the call of the drum spiritually, even when we're at an AC/DC concert. Drums are what humans do when they're worshipping, having fun, going to war, celebrating a wedding, welcoming a dignitary – you name it. Human beings are all about rhythm.

While the soundscape of Shamanic journeying is about rhythm and the spiritual significance behind that rhythm, it is also about energy. So, the tools and instruments discussed in this chapter serve a dual purpose:

- Creating a spiritual soundscape to facilitate a shift in consciousness
- Manipulating energy for the sake of spiritual and intellectual clarity

Of course, different strokes for different folks! And the point of using sound in Shamanism is to move between the material world and that of the spirits to derive wisdom, support, and healing from the ancestors and guides there. And if binaural beats work for the practitioner in this respect, they have fulfilled their appointed function.

Now that the book has given our position away on the question, let's examine some traditional tools and instruments employed by Shamans to shift their consciousness to the trance state.

Leaf Rattle

The leaf rattle is used in Latin American Shamanic traditions, particularly those found in the Amazon. Made from palm leaves dried and bound together, the sound made by this instrument is considered "*puro sonido*" (pure sound) by Amazonian Shamans.

This sound is said to convey the intentions of the Shaman.

Made from the leaves of a plant, the leaf rattle bears the tradition of union with nature on which Shamanism, wherever it is, is based. That's why the sound is considered pure. Human intervention has re-created a naturally occurring portion of a living tree as an article to facilitate spirituality. The leaf rattle is considered the most important tool used by Amazonian Shamans.

As the Shaman deploys the leaf rattle, the action of the hand becomes automatic. The Shaman detaches from the intention to deliberately shake the rattle, letting his hand do what it will do as the intention is focused. The mind/body complex collaborates with the rattle, acting as a natural element working with a human agent to disperse dense ambient energy and create a specific type of sound – that of dry leaves rustling.

Frame Drum

Frame drum.

Central to the project of entering the trance state of consciousness, the frame drum is common to all shamanic societies in various forms. Primarily informed by cultural context, the shape of the drum is round, with a frame of varying sizes and depths.

The sound of the drum is one we all know. We know it in almost every existing form of music. From humanity's earliest times, the drum, struck with the hand or a second instrument, has been a constant in every age and every place. Our most common legacy is the human body in all its permutations. But surely the second most common and most ancient is the drum. Without the drum, how would we dance and why? Without the guiding rhythm of the drum, when would our feet fall and rise? Without the guiding meter set by the drum, we would be lost on the dance floor.

And in Shamanism, the drum fulfills exactly that role, guiding the Shaman to the trance state of consciousness. In that state, the Shaman is prepared to enter and experience the spirit world on behalf of the community. Through the drum rhythms, the Shaman transitions to consciousness, enabling an epic journey of the soul. That journey is the journey both of humanity and the drum, uniting to breach the veil for the sake of all Creation.

The drum has always been with us, and the ceremonial frame drum of global Shamanism continues that human tradition. The larger drums are made of rawhide and wood, preferred by most Shamans due to their resonance.

Wrist and Ankle Rattles

Adding to the soundscape created by the frame drum (and the leaf rattle in the Amazon) are wrist and ankle rattles made from leather thongs and a variety of shells, including the sacred cowrie in African Shamanic cultures.

As a Shaman prepares to journey, the sound bears forth intention. All instruments used in Shamanic trance are intended to do so. Depending on the intentions of the Shaman, for healing, to settle a community matter, or to seek other spiritual counsel, the wrist and ankle rattles are deployed to provide autonomously driven sound. These rattles move as the Shaman moves through the soundscape, creating the music of intention.

Rattles may also be suspended from the ears, or tied around the waist or back, depending on the intention of being taken to the spirit world. The Shaman may do an ecstatic dance to the point of collapse, at which time the trance has been achieved.

Voice

The voice is as much an instrument as any created by humans. Of divine design, the human voice is the instrument built into our bodies and one of humanity's earliest means of self-expression and storytelling.

In concert with human-made instruments, the voice adds the sound of the speaking being, collaborating to create a soundscape that expresses human hope, transforming it into a phenomenon. Intention becomes more than a thought in the sounds produced to bear it forth to the spirit world. That phenomenon is a temporary fixture in the world, but its sources are material, driven by the spirit, which is both embodied and created by the embodied. That symbiosis is supernatural in the Shamanic context.

That symbiosis is primordial. The power of the human voice is evident to all living people. Its sound can break or heal hearts, destroy civilizations, or raise up empires. When heard, it is an almost material thing, embodying the intentions of the human it issues from just as the other instruments producing the soundscape of Shamanic ritual do.

Shamanic ritual music relies on no libretto or songs handed down. The intention decides on the sounds that come, the words that come, and the rhythms that come. The intention of the Shaman is the song. At times, as the ceremony progresses, Shamans may exhibit glossolalia (speaking in tongues) as they contact the spirits. This is the spirit world speaking through the Shaman. But the greeting is not intended to be understood. It is simply a signification of things to come, signaling the advent of a message the community has anticipated as the result of the ceremony.

Shamanic Container

The Shamanic container, which is obviously a modern term), is a space in which energies are manipulated. This is necessary to protect the ceremonial space from the incursion of any disruption by negative and other energies. Energetic interference can cause trance failure and the failure of intentions.

Further, in the instance of a healing ceremony, energies extraneous to the ceremony can insert themselves, shifting the intention and denying the person seeking spiritual healing agency, which is preeminent in a healing ceremony.

So, the Shamanic container is duly cleared of unwanted energies (rattles, drum, voice), dispersing them with collaborative sound. The space is cleared, and the energies of all concerned are protected in their intentions and supplications.

The establishment of a Shamanic container is crucial to the conduct of any Shamanic ritual, as energy is at the heart of Shamanism. Everything that exists, including us, consists of energy. So, the energy that is managed works with our intentions instead of against them. Deliberately and ritually clearing a space for the journey of the Shaman's spirit protects the intention driving the action, safeguarding the Shaman's reception of the spirit world's response.

Smudge Stick

White age smudge stick.

Paloma Cervantes, CC BY-SA 3.0 <https://creativecommons.org/licenses/by-sa/3.0>, via Wikimedia Commons: https://commons.wikimedia.org/wiki/File:White_sage_smudge_sticks.jpg

The smudge stick is another tool used to manage energies in the ritual space. Before we begin, we must say a word about the infamous and much sought-after white sage. For one, it is just sage. There is nothing special about white sage, except that it is sage, which has a sacred role in many Shamanic cultures, particularly those of North American First Peoples. We intend to contribute to an end to the over-harvesting of this beleaguered plant, which has been plundered in Southern California by commercial interests. White sage does not grow everywhere and has been part of the ritual life of peoples living near those areas it does grow in for millennia. But now, the plant's future is in jeopardy (see Resources section). Please do not add to the frenzy about white sage. It is not required for your purposes. Containing polyphenols, desert sage has antiseptic properties and is astringent, but even household sage can be used.

Sage is known as a cleanser and healer. It is used to disperse energies in specific spaces for specific purposes and has been known since ancient times. Its Latin root is a testament to its power: "*salvare*" (to save or to heal).

Growing Sage

Sage is an adaptable plant that is easy to grow! And common sage (*Selva Oficinialis*) is perfectly acceptable for use in a smudge, with many of the same properties as white sage (without the colonialist guilt).

Whether you plant it in a container or in your garden, sage is a reasonably low-maintenance plant. Start it in the spring or fall when the weather is relatively mild. Plant it at the time of the final frost or before the first frost, or 6 to 8 weeks earlier for both seasons, if you are planting inside.

Lightly cover your seeds with soil, placing them at a reasonable distance from each other to ensure healthy root establishment.

Sage loves direct sunlight, so ensure your plants are positioned where they will get 6 hours of sunlight daily. They should have shade in the afternoon if you live in a hotter climate. Sage has some resistance to drought, so don't over-water. Young plants should only need light watering, resulting in moist soil. As your plants mature, water to a depth of 1 to 2 inches and make sure not to get the leaves wet. Mildew is a danger if leaves are consistently wet.

See the Resources section for more information about how to grow and maintain your own supply of sage for making smudges. You will also find a tutorial there for creating your own smudge sticks.

The Medicine Wheel and the Four Cardinal Directions

Life is a cyclical affair. The seasons progress in their accustomed way, year after year. Our lives begin, cycling through their own seasons, and then end, starting yet another cycle. The aboriginal (primordial or original) concept of time isn't linear. It is cyclical, and the medicine wheel bears witness to the reality that this was once the common human way of interpreting time.

The Medicine Wheel appears in various indigenous cultures, but in North America, we usually associate it with the First Peoples of the continent (Turtle Island). The Mayan people's round calendar was highly elaborate but expressed time in the same way. The Wheel echoes the cyclical nature of the cosmos and all of its various systems, beginning at the end and ending at the beginning in an eternal loop. Time does not end or begin. We don't end or begin. There is only eternity, expressing the passage of time as an ever-revolving circle.

Within the Medicine, the Wheel is held in the Four Cardinal directions, north, south, east, and west. These directions are spiritual truths as well as physical ones, expressed as the colors white, yellow, red, and black. Each of these represents a stage within the human life cycle, the colors of humanity, and the seasons of the year. Each of the four also has an associated spirit animal about which we will talk shortly.

The Medicine Wheel stands as a message of our interconnectedness with nature and with time itself. The nature of human life and the diversity of humanity is expressed in the Wheel, tying it to Creation as an intimate participant in the unending cosmic drama.

In our next chapter, we will be going into much more detail about the Medicine Wheel and its role in reaching out to the spirit world for healing. But the centrality of this tool and symbol can't be understated. The Medicine Wheel is at the heart of Shamanic practice as the earliest expression of human spirituality. Because we knew only what we experienced directly, we also knew that we belonged there and that we had an important role to play. But the Medicine Wheel expresses that relationship as symbiotic. In the world of the Medicine Wheel, humanity is not a steward or an observer. Humanity is not "detached" or in a supervisory role. On the contrary, we are part of the Wheel, woven into it in all our colors and ages, eternally turning as part of the fabric of reality itself.

Next, let's explore the Medicine Wheel as an important Shamanic tool and guide for healing.

Chapter Four, Part I: The Medicine Wheel

The medicine wheel.

The Medicine Wheel shown above is traditional, appearing in various cultures with variations influenced directly by that context. But the form of the medicine wheel – and its message – are unchanging. Anchored by the Four Cardinal Directions, the seasons, and human life cycles, the Wheel is an eternal constant.

Our bodies bear witness to the truth of the Wheel in their own cycles. Our blood circulates continually, pumped by the heart. We consume and eliminate, consume and eliminate. Our cells are continually regenerated. We see this most poignantly in our hair and nails, which consist of dead cells. Continually growing, we cut our nails and hair, and they grow back.

The truth is that life is like that – cyclical. Even the scribes of the Christian Scriptures knew this truth, describing Jesus as the "Alpha and Omega," the beginning and the end. The Church itself is governed by the cycles of time, with the liturgies of the Church cycling through the Christian calendar, starting each year anew at the Easter Moment of resurrection.

The circle is all, and the Medicine Wheel expresses that eternal reality simply, in a format we can all understand and which is common knowledge to us all if we're only willing to consider the message.

Within the same eternal cycle are our ancestors, ever guiding us. In our knowledge of the Wheel is where they reside. Their lives having been governed by the same eternal cycle as our lives are, they walk among us in the context of the Wheel, reminding us that we're accompanied by those who went before and their wisdom.

This brings us to the 7 key lessons of the Medicine Wheel, which are crucial to understanding to penetrate the mysteries of this symbol and tool of Shamanism.

The Four Directions

As we discussed in the last chapter, the Four Cardinal Directions have spiritual and practical significance for human life. Beginning in the east, childhood is represented by the color yellow, symbolizing the life-giving warmth of the sun. This is the spring of life, in the air element, represented by the spirit animal, the eagle.

The eagle is charged with the delivery of prayer, rising to the Creator. The eagle is also the messenger of messages emanating from the Creator. This spirit animal is the communicator but also the keeper of key values like strength, vision, and courage, required to raise up the leaders of tomorrow and hoped for as part of their eventual character as adults. This Direction's plant is tobacco, offered in prayer and for the ancestors.

Moving clockwise around the wheel, the next Direction is south, representing youth and the glory of summer. Its color is red, associated with vitality and energy. Its associated element is earth, and the spirit animal of this part of life is the wolf.

The wolf ranges through nature, hunting to survive. The wolf is bold, loyal, strong, and independent. This is the hope for our youth; that they are prepared for the vagaries of life to overcome them with confidence. The spirit of the wolf guides the young to live up to their potential and prevail. The associated plant is cedar, also offered in prayer and considered sacred, particularly in Western Canadian First Nations societies.

Next, we move east, the quadrant of the Wheel associated with adulthood. The color associated is black, which is the combination of all colors and the synthesis of lessons learned in childhood and youth, and the season is autumn. The element associated is water, which both flows dispassionately and patiently wears down, which is both nurturing and destructive. In adulthood, we are given choices that can be acted upon because of our adult status. With the combined lessons of childhood and youth under our belts, it is hoped that adulthood will prepare us for our role as elders and the wisdom we associate with people at that stage of life.

The spirit animal associated with this Direction is the buffalo. The buffalo is a symbol of strength in unity and fulfills a special role in First Nations culture. Remembered as a source of food, clothing, weapons, and many other items, the buffalo has walked with First Nations people for millennia as a partner. In adulthood, we seek the strength of unity because we have learned that there is nothing that cannot be achieved within a community. We reject isolationism and individualism, cleaving to the community that sustains us. We have learned that we are part of something greater than ourselves. Sage is the sacred plant associated with the eastern Direction, its sweet scent cleansing, healing, and bearing up the prayers of the community.

Finally, the northern Direction is where the elders live. In First Nations societies, the elders are the source of guidance, closer to the spirit world than other humans. Having learned the lessons of life, the elder is uniquely placed to dispense wisdom, supporting the community with advice, direction, and reminders about what life is for - to be at one with all that is. The color of this direction is white, the absence of all color, representing the fullness of the human spirit as it prepares to graduate to the next human reality, physical death.

The elder stands at the crossroads between the material and spiritual worlds, reminding their respective communities that as they are now, so shall others be. Their role is not only to guide and counsel in this life but for the sake of the next life, where we will join our ancestors to support the activities of those yet living on this side of the veil. The element of this season is fire, symbolizing transformation and the proximity of the spirit world but also the flame of knowledge held by elders.

The bear is the spirit animal of the north and a symbol of rebirth in many First Nations cultures. This is due to the bear's hibernation in winter and "resurrection" in spring. In essence, the bear stands in this direction to guide the elders to their homes, where they will hibernate, eventually emerging again in the spring - just as the bear does. Sweetgrass is the plant for this Direction. The people of the Great Plains believe that it was the plant covering the earth at Creation. It is used as a spiritual cleanser, preparing people for prayers, meeting to discuss important matters and profound changes, and cleansing the energies of physical spaces and people.

The 4 Seasons

The 4 seasons correspond to the stages of human life and specifically to the Cardinal Directions. As has been elaborated above, the season is intimately tied to the seasons of our lives.

Spring relates to new life and to childhood. Under the sun, all things grow, including our children. They grow and learn and find their places, becoming youth, the season of life during which more complex explorations occur, analogous to summer. This season is related to the color red, vibrant, passionate, and alive with curiosity.

Adulthood is the fall of our lives. The leaves change color, the air grows crisp, and we synthesize what we've learned to transition to the season of the elder, winter. Winter is white, signifying the spiritual nature of old age and its wisdom. Death, in this model, is transition. Both goodbye and hello, death in the world of the Medicine Wheel is what we prepare for as elders in this final season of life. But as we are heading for the door, we leave behind the gifts of a life lived intentionally.

The Elements

Earth, fire, air, and water are the four familiar elements of the Medicine Wheel. We have discussed them briefly above, and, like the Directions and the seasons, they have unique wisdom to impart.

Being in the west, yellow is the color of spring. In First Nations cosmology, it is also the color of fire (surprise), bringing us light, growth, and warmth. But the element in play is air. The air we breathe bears the breath that animates us, the scents we know and those we don't. Air fills lungs and builds fires. Its invisible caprices govern our lives and those that reside in the spirit world. Air is both a material element and a bearer of spirit, melding elemental and spiritual power, resulting in the miracle of new life.

Next is the earth, which is red. From the earth grows what sustains us, including the medicine naturally offered by plants. The earth feeds us and heals us. Next is east, and the color black represents the element of water. Our bodies are principally comprised of water, and we can't live for more than a day without ingesting it. Water nourishes plants and animals and renews the earth. Finally, we come to winter, where we find fire.

Please recall that the color of spring is yellow, which signifies fire. In this connection is a tantalizing glimpse into the cosmology driving the shamanic practices of First Nations peoples. The fire of spring's warmth and light is the same fire that appears in its elemental form in winter, the season of old age. This connects the season of death to the season of birth/childhood with poignant clarity. This element's position in the winter quadrant is adjacent to that of birth/childhood on the Wheel.

And fire is the most evocative of all 4 elements. It is arguable that all 4 elements are deeply evocative and known to provoke our prolonged reflection. While that is a worthy argument, nothing quite captures the human imagination like fire. We were once so obsessed with fire that we learned to make it ourselves. You will understand the mental energy required by the curious ancient who invented human-generated fire if you have ever attempted to light one yourself – with a modern fire-producing implement – in the rain.

But it doesn't take much mental energy to see the fullness of elemental fire as the goal of childhood, illuminated by its brilliant, embracing color. To be an elder is not to be set aside as consumed. It is to be the fullness of the fire once promised.

Plants

In the east, we find tobacco, specifically offered to the Creator and to the ancestors. It is the primordial gift to the people of medicine. In the south, we find sage. Sage is an energetic cleanser that repels negativity and prepares people's spirituality for ritual and for oral history and teaching.

Next, sweetgrass is the plant of the east. This sacred plant is the first fruit of Creation, used as a purifying agent prior to rituals, in sacred spaces, and in the home. Cedar is located north of the Wheel and is a purifying agent that serves a similar purpose to sage, with the added advantage of repelling evil. Cedar is often used in First Nations cultures with sweat lodge traditions, which describes cultures in the southwest corner of Canada.

Spirit Animals

We will be talking more about these spiritual friends soon, but they are one of the lessons revealed in the Wheel, so here's a capsule version! Animals most commonly associated with the Medicine Wheel have already been discussed, but in some First Nation spiritualities, the white buffalo takes the bear's place. For some people, the animal is sacred. Bear, eagle, wolf, and buffalo are all featured on the Wheel for their significance to First Nations spirituality and for their energetic qualities. More about that soon!

The Heavens Above

We know that the sun rises in the east, so that is where it lives on the Medicine Wheel. When the sun comes up, a new day has begun, and it is time to get busy, and that's what this association is all about. In the south is our home, the Earth, positioned under the Heavens Above, in all their glory. Our home is a very special place, and humans have a special role to play in the whole.

In the west is the moon, lighting our way by night, governing the tides of oceans, and giving wing to the human soul in creativity. Magnetic and enigmatic, the moon reflects the light of the sun, shining benevolently.

In the north are the stars. In their splendor, they represent the ancestors and our unity with the spirit world as living beings who will one day divide the veil ourselves. The stars speak to us at night. They guide our way home.

The Seasons of Our Lives

The seasons of the Medicine Wheel are the seasons of our lives, so the final lesson of the Medicine Wheel is the most pointed – that humans are intimately enmeshed in the cosmic drama and its cycles. We are not observers or stewards. We are speaking beings in Creation, with a special mission of healing. Our mission is to be healed and to heal.

The Shaman stands at the center of human communities in the Shamanic traditions, leading the long-term project of healing the micro for the sake of the macro. What is done in the human community reverberates through Creation. Because, just as our lives are enmeshed in the Wheel of time, so is everything else. Just as our lives reach out for healing, so does everything else, and that is the mission of the Shaman to repair the torn fabric of Creation by healing within a specific community. From that, communal healing grows renewed life and extended healing.

The seasons of our lives and the seasons of time are linked on the Medicine Wheel within the elements, the plants, the animals, the colors, and the Cardinal Directions themselves. We are born adjacent to our eventual role, that of elders, and all life's seasons lead to that inevitable terminus. This is the intention of the

Wheel, to remind us of who we are and what we are to do, to heal and be healed, and to increase the healing we dispense and receive with active love.

In Part II of this chapter, we will talk about the Medicine Wheel and healing. Next, let's build on our understanding of the Medicine Wheel.

Chapter Four, Part II: Healing with the Medicine Wheel

Health is homeostasis, that is, balance throughout all the systems of the body. In First Nations' Shamanism, balance is described as the full health of the 4 pillars of holistic health: physical, spiritual, intellectual, and emotional. When one of these supportive pillars is unwell or in a state of decay, the others will soon follow.

We have read how the Medicine Wheel acts as a capsule guide to time and how the human being and the Creation it lives in proceed in the seasons of time. As speaking beings, we inhabit a specialized corner of Creation, lesser in some respects but greater in others. We are like other creatures in that respect within this animistic cosmology, but we have a specific role tied to our ability to speak, organize, and think in abstract, creative ways.

And these cognitive and communicative abilities lie a double-edged sword, and so, through time, the Medicine Wheel has arisen as a codification of knowledge gathered generationally and passed down to us. The Wheel tells the tale of time and how we are enmeshed in its cycles, similar to threads woven into a whole cloth.

Finding Balance

Balance within the self is taught to those who listen to the world around them. Just as the Medicine Wheel guides our steps through the seasons of life, it stands as an intimate reminder of the natural world's family status. In the cosmology of all shamanisms, nature is the ground of the human creature wherever they are. This is reflected in the Hebrew Creation narrative, with humanity formed from the dust. We know we are not in Creation as its master but as a partner, grooming, trimming, fattening, and thinning. The human hand is charged with applying the balance taught by nature, allowing what has grown tired to go fallow and what has grown fat to harvest.

But living as most of us do in this age, we forget our place. We cleave to ideologies of human domination and build towers of Babel at the slightest provocation. Do you know where the tallest building on Earth is located? Neither do many people – and yet they build them taller every year. And we stop knowing who we are and where we're from as we zip around the globe like manic fireflies, looking for just the right flower. Nature is only of interest when there's a benefit to us.

The growing interest in Shamanism is all the proof you need that what I just wrote is true. We are hungry and thirsty for something to fill the chasm of vapidity that lives within us, never satisfied in the absence of true sustenance. We fill it with Kardashians and ketchup brands, cabbages, and kinks. It's all boring, but we eat it and like it. But what do we really want?

We want the real thing. We want the forgotten balance of our lives. We want to be liberated from unhealthy obsessions and petty resentments. We want a way forward. We want a way – any way – out of this emptiness. People looking to Shamanism to fill that gaping inner void are starting on the right foot. There is healing to be had here, starting with yourself. You have lived in the society that this chapter is talking about. Drained of all meaning save the primacy of the individual, nothing satisfies. That may be the reason that you are here – *and certainly, the reason this book is being written.*

You are here to find the balance that is your human birthright. Homeostasis is your human legacy, and the Medicine Wheel offers a way to begin the process of restoring it. The Medicine Wheel may be represented as a talisman, but it's more of a road map for making the most of your brief human life on this earth.

Getting to "Healed"

You may not be a fan of "silver bullets." You may not care for simple answers to complex questions. So, it's only fair to tell you that healing is a long-term project. There's nothing easy about it, and the Medicine Wheel is not your silver bullet. There is no such thing when it comes to establishing wholeness in your human organism.

Healing is a journey, and most of your healing happens as you move towards that moment you hope for – the moment of complete freedom in healing. Few of us get there, truth be told. But our wounds are noble, and when we allow them to speak to us, sharing with us the wisdom we missed while we were angry and depressed about the misfortune of hurt, we move a step closer.

The Shaman, as we have learned, is one with a wound. The Wounded Healer comes to us as one who has no shame in the wound, using it as an open door for others to walk through. This truth speaks to the nobility of the wound from your standpoint. Not everything can be healed, as we might like to believe. It may be transformed into something else instead. We may not see whatever that is coming, but life is like that. Life is how it is, not how we desire it to be.

Ultimately, self-healing is the first imperative of one who aspires to heal others, so it is important that you be as brutally honest with yourself as possible. Where are your wounds? What caused them? At what time of life did they occur? Which of these wounds is the one that might mean a vocation?

If you are going to approach the Medicine Wheel honestly, with integrity, and without preconceived ideas about what you are learning from it, you are going to gain wisdom and strength from experience. If you're not going to do that, then it's best to do nothing.

Healing yourself in as conscious a way as you can is your journey into another way of seeing the Medicine Wheel and its role in guiding human life and action is the project. Pursuing this method of healing is a means of rediscovering the human relationship to nature and the riches of what that rediscovery holds out to you.

The Map of Your Soul

See in the Medicine Wheel what it truly represents. It is a map of your soul. You are a creature living in Creation, echoing the cycles of the earth. You live and die and regenerate.

The Wheel is a picture of who you are and who you are meant to be. It is a guide to living consciously, neither valuing one part of life nor devaluing another. In this world, young is not better than old, any more than the east is better than the north. The Wheel is a picture of a balanced human body, mind, spirit, and emotions. All are equally important. All are part of you. All these parts of you deserve an equal measure of your loving ministrations and attention.

You are more than flesh, but you are also a self-contained and complex affair. And modernism (and these days, post-modernism) has increasingly brought into question what it means to be a human being. But part of everyone alive remembers their true humanity, on some level. We all have a faint impression. Sometimes all it takes is a visual aid and a philosophical framework to help us remember the details as they were and are.

The Number Four

In case you hadn't noticed, the number 4 figures prominently in the world of the Medicine Wheel. There are 4 directions, 4 seasons, 4 colors, 4 animals, and 4 plants. There are 4 stages of human life. And in that human life, what constitutes balance is the equal potency of body, mind, spirit, and emotion. In this balanced state, these elements of the human organism have a distinct place and a role to play. One is not suffering neglect due to another being centered. This is the happy family model of the human being in good (balanced) working order.

It is further said, in this cosmology, that life's cycles may be further reduced to 4-year periods of growth. And this is key learning – that our lives, lived in the knowledge that 4 years is the length of our human cycles of growth and learning, might be happier and less anxiously restless. When we understand the cyclical nature of human life in the context of the Medicine Wheel, these 4-year cycles begin to make themselves apparent to us, serving to contain our aggressive demand for more of everything "right now."

Reflect-Pray-Confront

The form of the medicine wheel, in its symmetry and meaning, is made for contemplative interaction. The richness of this incredible tradition invites you into its mysteries, and your story is woven into the fabric of Creation as an essential thread or part of it.

Coming to the Medicine Wheel as a way of healing is not transmissible via formula. Due to the traditional status of the Wheel, it's there for everyone to learn the dialogue and use it as a tool for healing. The prerequisite is *respect,* and being true to the Wheel's role as a guide for living well.

Let's examine the components of approaching the Medicine Wheel as spiritual support and guide to life.

Reflect

Within the Wheel's sacred circle, the 4 Directions speak their truths, and you speak yours in an interactive exchange of mutual sharing. As you contemplate the Wheel, be aware of events in your life that correspond to the 4 Seasons and the Directions in which they are found:

- New ventures – East
- Marital difficulties – West
- Aimlessness – South
- Concerns with illness; death obsessions – North

The examples shown above are presented for illustrative purposes only, but you need to understand why they are located in the Directions shown, so you can do the same with your own life questions and areas in need of healing:

- New ventures belong in the east, as this is the Direction of spring and new beginnings (child)
- Marital difficulties are in the western direction of fall and the part of life in which our efforts come to fruition (adult)
- Aimlessness is situated in the south, where summer indolently reigns (youth)
- Illness and death obsessions belong in the northern quadrant, as this is where the winter of life renders wisdom and knowledge (elder)

It may not seem simple to boil down your life concerns and wounds in need of healing following what has been offered above, but you'll learn with time. As you become more adept at naming your woundedness, you'll discover that you have become more adept at locating it in the appropriate quadrant. With the support of the spirit guides and your own radical honesty, the Wheel becomes a fellow traveler on the way. You determine the quality of your dialogue with the Medicine Wheel. When that quality is determined by the purity of intent and your own honesty, your healing will manifest in numerous constructive ways.

Name your wound or wounds. Understand why they have brought you to the Wheel for healing, and seek in the message of the Directions and the Wheel's other elements the place to seek its sutures. You will come to know the Wheel when you approach it as a dialogue and not a monologue. Projecting yourself onto the wheel as you are will only confuse the interaction. Instead, go as a stranger to yourself and to the Wheel. Go as a seeker, and you will find the healing you desire.

Pray

You will not pray to the Wheel. You will pray in the presence of and under the guidance of the Wheel. Remember that humanity created the Medicine Wheel to express the nature of the reality we live in. From the observation of the ancestors, the Medicine Wheel was born as a sacred road map, creating a nexus of spirituality that told the dramatic story of an interconnected Creation.

When you pray intending to find healing within the world of the Wheel, you will tell your story to yourself, to the spirit world, to the animals, the plants, and the elements. You will speak your truths and, in them, commune with what you're an indelible part of. Most of us have forgotten our role as threads in the fabric of Creation. In remembering that part of your reality, you will become something more and something less at the same time. Being part of something precludes the egoism of individuality, overtaking your humanity (which is communal).

Recovering that crucial memory, the memory of humanity reunited with the wholeness of the creature's truth, is healing. While it may not close the whole wound or all the wounds you have, it breathes hope into you. The Wheel breathes into you a distant memory of balance in Creation and in your soul, now distorted by realities you didn't create.

And in the Medicine Wheel, as you pray with the intention for the gift of healing, you will find the guide that has always been there, waiting for you to discover it.

Confront

To recover the fullness of your humanity in spirit, confrontation is required. Any quest for healing is incomplete if we fail to confront ourselves and our participation in the woundedness from which we are trying to recover. What have we done? What haven't we done? What might we do? What do we want to do? Why are we here?

Confronting yourself as a human creature is getting to the root of the wound. It is reaching into the wound and pulling from it the pus and decay that have allowed it to prosper and proliferate within you. This isn't about blaming trauma, ill fortune, or poor health on yourself. This is about finding in yourself the way to the core, where the wound was made. Finding that out is the next step toward healing.

If you don't know the source, how can you trust what you think you know? If you aren't sure about where things come from, do you really want to buy them? It's the same with finding the source of your wound. You can't heal the malady without understanding how it was contracted. The sources of our wounds are key information we need to close them.

Pain is not something most of us look forward to confronting. We prefer to bury the pain, just as we bury a lot of worldly garbage. That doesn't work either, we have learned. Burying pain is a modern convenience in a busy world, which has no time for your pain or anyone else's.

To confront your pain, though, is to dig into that wound, clearing it of the rot that prevents it from closing and healing. It's that rot, unpleasant as it is, that you must stick your delicate pinkie in and clean to heal.

Graphic Healing

The Medicine Wheel is a concise graphic representation of Creation and the speaking being's intimate role in and relationship with it. The seasons of Creation are the seasons of our lives, the animals, our friends, and exemplars, among all the planet's lavish gifts for our use. Reflecting on the 7 lessons of the Medicine Wheel helps us place our wounds in perspective, accepting the past as another turn of the Wheel. Time moves in a circle and never stops doing so, despite what happens in our lives. These things happen in all our lives and always have. The Wheel doesn't stop to make a note of the reliable and immutable. It turns, inviting us to explore time and its wounds from an ancient, organic perspective, a perspective that has existed since the dawn of the Homosapien.

In the Medicine Wheel is the hope of a new approach to spirituality that re-writes the human story as part of a much bigger one and, in so doing, creates an ordered graphic world rich with meaning, intimacy, and traditional sacred knowledge. Employing the graphic world of the Medicine Wheel is a very personal experience. It is a journey of recovered connections, renewed balance, and healed wounds. We come to ourselves in many diverse ways, and with the Wheel, we come to the story of humanity's closest family – Creation itself.

The evocative, graphic quality of the wheel is a testament to the human intellect and its ability to synthesize vast concepts into color, a direction, an animal, or a plant. Creating such synthesis is the work of generations, calling to each other across time for the sake of healing.

The Medicine Wheel is a road map and teacher, rewarding our efforts to understand Creation and our place in it with healing and simple, supportive guidance. The Medicine Wheel will not describe your personality type or diagnose your personality disorder. The Medicine Wheel is going to help you come to terms with where you have been, who you are and where you are going. The Wheel knows the seasons of your life as its own. You share a heartbeat, and that intimacy is the basis for your spiritual dialogue.

Human hands created the fruit of human minds and human observation in the Medicine Wheel. The truth was made for us to see and grow from, and the Wheel tells that profound but simple truth rooted in the material world and its inhabitants.

Next, let's meet the spirits of nature in our animal and plant cousins. Who are they, and how can we work with them?

Chapter Five: Spirit Animals and Shamanic Plants and Allies

In an animist tradition, the centrality of the human-animal gives way to encompass other agents of Divine Will. The natural world looms, not as a wild enemy to be tamed then exploited but to be lived with in appreciation.

Remembering that animism posits a universal soul infusing all that is, it's not hard to understand why respect for the natural world is pivotal to a philosophy that doesn't dominate but walks parallel. To Westerners, this may seem strange. Our philosophies teach us that the Earth was given for us to "subdue" if we follow the imperatives of the Creation story in the Book of Genesis.

But the idea of animism validates the sacredness of all that is animate and inanimate, visible and invisible, as it all bears the imprint of the Divine. In this model, it's not just ever-so-clever humanity benefiting from a Divine infusion. It's the ground we so carelessly walk on, pave over and dig up in our presumed primacy.

Concerning spirit animals, we should define the term. "Spirit animal" in this chapter refers to "power animal" and "totem animal." These terms are interchangeable, and the term "spirit animal" best defines the role of animal spirit actors as guides, supporters, friends, and teachers.

The Shamanic tradition brings the spirits of sacred plants and animals to our sides, providing powerful allies that join our ancestors in guiding us. Let's start with an overview of some of the better-known spirit animals.

Spirit Animals

The spirit animal's role is most coherent to the Western mind when described as a guardian angel. Everyone has a spirit animal, bringing us a source of reflective empowerment rooted in the animal's attributes.

The spirit animal brings us protection from illness and misfortune so that when a guardian leaves us, as will happen throughout our lives, we are exposed but only briefly. The spirit animal is as cyclical as our lives, coming to teach us, then leaving to make space for the next teacher.

Our list will serve as an introduction to spirit animals, but I should clarify that any animal can be a spirit animal, including insects and reptiles (see Resources for a guide to finding your personal spirit animal). Because of their sacred role, we will start our discussion with the animals associated with the quadrants of the Medicine Wheel.

Bear

Both feared and admired, the bear is an animal of unique attributes. Hibernating through the winter months, the bear has evolved to sleep and awaken as almost a resurrection (see Chapter 4, Spirit Animals).

The size of this animal, especially the monolithic Grizzly and the Kodiak, is enough to strike fear in the heart of humans, but a glimpse of the bear's fangs stops that heart short. The bear isn't deliberately aggressive; it defends what it needs to with its size and fangs. The bear has no problem reminding humans who has the edge in a fair fight!

Courage, the promise of life in spirit, and leadership are all part of the bear's spiritual persona.

Eagle

We all know the eagle soars, its eyes ever attuned to the movement of potential prey. The eagle is just as intimately connected to intellect as to spirit, uniting the two in the air element. Swift and decisive, the eagle soars gracefully in freedom.

The subject of human fancy, the eagle, is commonly associated with freedom from tyranny and mental toughness, focus, and vision. The independence of the eagle is widely admired by humans, demanding little but prey to exist entirely on its own terms.

Clear, concise vision, focus on achieving goals, and earning one's ultimate freedom are the teachings of the eagle, who reminds us that anything worth having is worth putting in the elbow grease for.

Buffalo

When the mighty buffalo isn't tossing tourists like a salad, this spirit animal stands as a symbol of abundance, evident in the sheer physical bulk that once fed nations. But the buffalo is also a strong symbol of hospitality, generosity, and survival.

When blessed with the sacred power of this spirit animal, the path of the holy is indicated. The buffalo comes to teach the patience of life in a difficult landscape, triumphing in resolute strength. The buffalo meets challenges head-on, butting against them until they scream, "Uncle!".

Wolf

While the wolf may not share much DNA with humans, it lives in a remarkably similar way, its social organizations, hierarchies, and family systems resembling our own. But the wolf is a misunderstood animal, often depicted as bloodthirsty and dangerous.

The wolf's role is to help us to understand the importance of our human instincts and to reconnect with them. Their value to us in life is priceless, and the wolf is the master of instinct. The wolf also counsels in the matter of getting where we want to go with confidence, following established rules of navigation that demand patience, a virtue of the stealthy wolf.

The wolf heals the heart by teaching that community is where we establish it, teaching us to take only what we need and to value the power of connection.

The Wolf is a spirit animal.
https://pxhere.com/en/photo/1441553

We have concentrated on these four animals because of their sacred status and their positions on the Medicine Wheel. But please don't stop with these. Check the Resources section for more on spirit animals. In the meantime, let's look at working with spirit animals generally and how they can help you.

Working with Spirit Animals

Review the descriptions above and ask yourself: "What do I need right now?" What is missing in the days of your life from your work, friendships, romantic relationship, hobbies, ambitions – whatever sector you can think of? What do you feel could really use a boost, and what qualities could be implicated in achieving that boost?

Depending on the answers to those questions, look to the guardian angels of the Wheel or their counterparts for guidance. What they can teach you is beyond anything you might have imagined!

But remember, spirit animals are exactly what they sound like. They are the spiritual counterparts of the material animals they represent. They are the spiritual flip side of their material realities, as all inhabitants of the spirit world are. Where once they lived in the flesh, they now live in the spirit, or perhaps as archetypes, symbolizing the animal in its spiritual aspects.

The spirit animal can communicate with you in numerous ways, including in your dialogues with the Medicine Wheel. If you have embarked on these, you will already have an idea of where some of the work you need to do is. You may even know which spirit animal is on board for this cycle. But you're learning, so stay alert. Be aware of the presence of the characteristics of your spirit animal. These are exemplary when seen in everyday examples such as advertisements on a bus or train or the words of a colleague or friend. Once you open yourself to the work of the spirit, you will begin to enter the synchronicity of the parallel existence of the spirit world. Approach with respect and be aware of the energy you are bringing to dialogue with the Medicine Wheel and your and other spirit animals. Cleanse yourself before entering the dialogue. Cleanse the space. Cleanse your heart and mind. To be in a relationship with your spirit animals is to be in a relationship with your primordial family and with the power of which we are all part.

Shamanic Plants and Allies

Before we begin, we need to clarify that this chapter does not recommend ingesting any of the plants mentioned without prior approval from a medical advisor. Further, such use should only be pursued under the guidance and direction of an experienced Shaman.

The plants of Shamanic traditions may vary from place to place, but there are constants. For our purposes, we'll stick to what's familiar for the sake of getting a foundation you can build on.

We already discussed plants briefly in Chapter 4, Part I. Here, we would like to talk a little more about the sacred significance of some other Shamanic plant allies and how they act as supporters and friends in our spiritual journeys.

Plant Spirit Shamanism

Animism, as we have discussed, posits everything, animate and inanimate, seen and unseen, to be infused with the Divine spirit.

Plants, of course, are not exceptions from this universal spiritual infusion. And some plants serve a special role as allies to human beings.

Plant Spirit Shamanism is even older than the shamanic traditions we have been reading about in this book. This is humanity's first connection to spirituality, embodied in the green shoots that grow from the earth, the flowers, the fungi, the mosses, and the roots. The Plant Spirit Shaman is said to derive power from the plants, which are the allies of humanity, speaking through the Wounded Healer in love.

In this section, we would like to introduce you to some ally plants you certainly know about but perhaps haven't yet thought of as allies in the Shamanic Journey. As you read, please be aware that few of today's Shamans partake of these substances, using sound as their means of crossing through the veil to non-ordinary reality.

Ayahuasca

Interest in Ayahuasca is not necessarily linked to interest in Shamanism. Certainly, the Beatles latched onto guru culture in the 1960s, so, naturally, the promise of a high that conveys one's spirit to the vast chambers of the Divine might attract a few with little genuine interest in spirituality. Not that there is anything wrong with that but getting high to have experiences intended for spiritual edification is not the subject of this book. We are talking about sacred plants for sacred purposes.

Ayahuasca is the bark of a vine found in the Amazon and is known for its hallucinogenic properties. The bark is boiled, and the resulting reduction is consumed. This is one way of conducting the Shamanic Journey

But Ayahuasca is an ally, reaching into the human soul to correct its course, open doors, and heal wounds. Of course, this is the work of the Shaman, the Wounded Healer appointed to join forces with the elements of nature to heal, correct, illuminate, and teach.

When the Shaman communes with Ayahuasca, the communion is one of essential spirits, uniting in common purpose. Because Ayahuasca, like all other things, is infused with the spirit of the Divine, in turn infusing the Shaman with its singular knowledge.

To consume Ayahuasca, the Shaman prepares by adjusting their customary diet, ensuring that everything consumed is naturally derived and free of contamination. Pursuing a diet in preparation also prepares the Shaman by undergirding intention. The application of a discipline before a spiritual or ritual action is known to have this effect, centering the mind on the work to come.

As stated above, Ayahuasca is a sacred plant that should never be consumed on a whim or for the sake of entertainment. This plant should always be consumed in the presence of a Shaman who consents to the action and conducts any associated rites.

Cannabis

Once demonized and prohibited, this famous herb has become a fixture in homes in many states in the USA and all of Canada and is on the cusp of being federally legalized in Mexico. All around the world, cannabis is being embraced as a helper and a friend. What Shamanic cultures have known for millennia, we are only just waking up to.

The Shaman deploys cannabis for a variety of purposes. One is healing, especially in the event of depression and other mental health challenges. Another is building connections (sacred bonds) between individuals and communities. Cannabis is also used to secure peace between warring factions. Some shamanic cultures also use cannabis as a funerary plant, covering the deceased's body with cannabis leaves to infuse the plant's power into the body as the soul departs on its next adventure.

The friendly cannabis plant has been given to humanity as a helper. It helps us relax, unplug from our busy days, and allow our creativity to come to the fore. It is medicine, a healer, and a life partner. But it also has a sacred purpose. Of the three plants discussed here, only cannabis has a recreational role. While the other two plants may be used recreationally, such use has nothing to do with Shamanism.

Peyote

Button cactus used in Latin American Shamanism.
Dav Hir, CC BY-SA 3.0 <https://creativecommons.org/licenses/by-sa/3.0>, via Wikimedia
Commons: https://commons.wikimedia.org/wiki/File:Lophophora_williamsii_Bl%C3%BCte.JPG

Most of us know about peyote, the small button cactus used in Latin American Shamanism. We may even have read Peruvian author Carlos Castaneda's accounts of his encounters with a Shaman name Don Juan. And most of us know that the Apache First Nations of the USA implicate peyote in their Shamanic rites.

Most readers won't know about the Wixarika, dubbed "Huichol" by the Mexica people, the pre-colonial rulers of the area which is today the United Mexican States. Unfortunately, the colonizing Spanish had no context for the word (which was insulting) and adopted it. The use of Huichol to describe the Wixarika had endured until recent times when the People finally regained their birth name.

Living in the mountainous areas of Jalisco state, the Wixarika retain their pre-Columbian beliefs and traditions to this day. They have resisted the proselytizing efforts of Roman Catholicism and the decaying influence of modernism. The name Wixarika means "healer," and the sacred peyote plant is at the center of this ancient people's belief system.

As we have discussed, the primary object of Shamanism is healing, and in the name of this, people are the truth. The community is united in the action to which it has been ordained – *healing*. This, and the steadfast refusal to be subsumed under the onslaught of colonialism and its enabling religious arm, is a testament to the incredible power of the Wixarika. The peyote cactus plays a tremendous role in that power.

That spiky little cactus at the center of Wixarika culture is psychoactive because it contains Mescaline, producing hallucinogenic effects. The framework for our thoughts is shifted, our self-awareness is radically altered, and time loses meaning. Senses are heightened, and reality allows itself to be seen in spiritually revealing ways.

Again, as stated earlier with Ayahuasca, the sacred nature of this natural substance precludes sourcing it for recreational purposes. The role of peyote is spiritual. This spiky, potent little friend is not to be trifled with, and again, a Shaman should be present to direct the experience if you plan to pursue ingesting peyote.

Shamans use these principal "ally plants" to achieve their journeys. In the next chapter, we will discuss clearing a ceremony space. This is primarily concerned with manipulating energy to prepare the appointed area for ritual purposes.

Chapter Six: Clearing Space for Ceremony

Animism's appeal to the spirit dwelling within everything that exists points to a fundamental truth about existence: everything is made of energy. Einstein famously said it, and as time passes, more of us are becoming interested in how energy affects the conduct of our daily lives.

Energy can't be seen. It can be felt. It can be intuitively recognized. And those who can feel and discern its quality are connected to the energetic reality of existence in a way that most of us aren't.

But all of us once were. There was once a time before the disruption of our senses and sleep cycles caused by electric light and ambient noise and the advent of the television and mass media – when we were much more sensitive to the energies in play around us. We feel less and less. We intuit less and less. We are less and less.

This is the gift of Shamanism to the modern world, to renew its senses by connecting them once again to the truth of spirit and the role of the human being as just another moving part (albeit as crucial as any other and with a significant role to play) in its diverse network of systems. The intention is to once again sense and feel *without social stigma* and to trust our intuition and instincts as we once did . . . to restore humanity to homeostatic health.

Healing is done by healers. The Wixarika are called "the healers," presenting the community as having a specific role on the earth. Their entire identity is held in that role, and Shamanism, while as diverse as Creation itself, is always concerned with healing the human being, the community, and its relationships. Healing is the mission of Shamanism, and that healing is achieved in various ways – one of which is ceremony.

Wounded to Renew

The Shaman as Wounded Healer bears a clue. We must learn to embrace the pain to renew the ability to trust our most primal capacities (instinct and intuition). Pain occurs when we love. Love is never given or received without this shadow lingering to one side of it.

To love is to give oneself to another, to a cause, to oneself, to Creation, to the community, or to a passion, with all that you are. Love is total commitment. So, when pain comes, the commitment of love is metastasized, transforming as the fullness of the love you have given reveals its other face. Loss is pain. Separation is pain. Rejection is pain. Hatred is pain. When pain comes to love, it comes as a shock to the system, a rude awakening.

But that same pain comes to rend the heart open, gripping it with icy claws that lay it bare to release its fullness. In pain's rude invasion of love is the wound that renews. In the silence of contemplation and the humility of surrender to any of our ally plants or to the comforting spirits of those who came before or our guiding animals comes the true love, broken and renewed in all its wounded glory.

You may not have a vocation to be a Shaman, but, as the great Leonard Cohen once wrote, understand that a crack is how the light gets in. The broken heart releases its fullness, making room for that which has been lost, damaged, and repaired. It's in a shamanic way, practiced for the good of yourself and the community you live in so that you may regain and reconnect with the human superpower of intuition. The broken heart is where these amazing human abilities are reborn.

Intuition and Energy

Intuition is a magnificent human gift. Instinct precedes it as the vestigial work of the amygdala, where the "flight or fight" response is found, telling us to run from that predator. It was effective for primitive men. But for the fully evolved Homosapien, instinct on its own is perhaps too reactive or too ready to bop a nose at the drop of a hat.

And so, we have intuition, which is far more refined. Intuition is the voice within, giving us information to consider. Reason intercedes, whispering, "Take a breath." Serving intuition to ensure it has analyzed the situation (a feeling about a situation, an opportunity, a person, a job, you name it), reason applies what it knows to intuition, advising and regulating it to process the information provided by that inner voice.

Intuition is the seat of our ability to discern the nature of energy around us. It is a superpower that tips us off to imminent events, informed by the logical deduction provided by our friend, reason. Intuition helps us size up tonight's date and tomorrow's job interview. It tells us why that person is sad. It tips us off that the guy at the bus stop is shady. Intuition helps us live our lives undisturbed by the things we don't need in it. It saves us from a lot of suffering.

So why don't most of us listen to it? Simply put: we live in an empirically obsessed world that actively discounts the role of intuition. It wants to see the data. If you don't have the data, there is nothing to discuss. Intuition in the post-emotional (and, to be honest, post-human) 21st Century is obsolete.

This is how malignant narcissists, psychopaths, and sociopaths prosper. Because most of us ignore intuitive internal messaging, we don't see these corrosive beings coming. Some of us even marry them, ignoring all the red flags intuition has warned us with because "that's just nonsense."

Intuition is an early warning system. When we listen to it, allowing its voice to guide us, we can avoid some of life's worst pitfalls. When we ignore it, we fall into the pit like prey.

What intuition is sensing is energy. We emit it. We are made of it. And when we interact with other people, we exchange it. We share our energies with those we're in contact with, for better or worse. Understanding our inner voice and listening to it takes practice, but we all have the capacity.

Heeding Intuition

Listening to your inner voice is a learned behavior. We can all name incidents when intuition spoke to us from our very core. We all can remember times when we have ignored our intuition or when we have heeded - and the events that followed in both examples.

So, right now, take a moment to think of the times in your life when you have ignored your intuition and regretted it. Write them down. Think about the factors that led you to ignore your inner voice. Was it something someone said? Did you feel a silly feeling that way about the situation? Were you afraid your inner voice was wrong?

Now, write down the times in your life when you haven't ignored your intuition. What convinced you to listen? What was the outcome? Was it better or worse? If worse, was that really your inner voice, or were you bargaining with yourself from the ego?

Getting a handle on your inner voice and making friends with it must happen before you can even hope to clear a space for a ceremony. It is your intuition that is most tightly connected with the spirit world. You are most connected to the energetic realities around you through your intuition. You can't see the energy, but in the material world, you can see its source. When you listen to your intuition, even when you can't immediately see the source, you will eventually see it.

Practice listening to your inner voice. Talk to it. Take a breath and listen. When questions or challenges arise in your life, allow your inner voice to speak. Allow it to counsel and then weigh what you have heard against what you know (reason). The result is forging a connection with your intuitive superpower that will allow you to freely discern and sense energies around you, both materially and spiritually based. That ability is crucial to enable you to find your way toward your place in Creation as one of its human components, working with it, for it, and for your community, even if that's just your apartment block or workplace; you will find plenty of people in need of healing in both places.

When you renew your human superpower, you will experience a profound shift in the way you sense the world around you and, eventually, the way you sense its energies, those of other human beings and of the spirits, ancestors, and spirit animals.

Matter and Energy in Balance

The Shamanic concept of matter and energy posits that energy affects the material. Of course, it does. Everything is made of energy, so how could that not be? That's especially true of "unseen energy." While energy, as a rule, can't be seen, "unseen" in this instance has a very specific meaning.

These energies represent those things we carry within us that remain unresolved. Trauma is generally the source, and trauma is prevalent in our society, so none of us gets off this planet unscathed by it. It's the way of a world that's out of balance. The imbalance in the world, provoked by human activity, also resides in our lives and souls. The work of Shamanism seeks to realign these energies, not by "positive thinking" or "trying to do better at life," but by directly addressing the energetic imbalance many of us unknowingly live with.

Koyaanisqatsi

While the Hopi People no longer practiced Shamanism, this was their traditional way at one time. Their unique worldview and language captured the attention of documentary filmmakers in 1982, resulting in the film Koyaanisqatsi. This Hopi word means "life out of balance." If you haven't seen this film, it is strongly recommended as a visual representation of the energetic imbalance which has led us to this contemporary state of the world. Four decades ago, the film prophetically warned that imbalance has severe consequences, a reality we're seeing the truth of as the earth's climate changes and extreme weather holds human lives in its grip. We have included a link to the documentary in the Resources section.

This word gives us a glimpse into the now abandoned traditions of the Hopi, pointing to its former Shamanic framework. Life out of balance, Koyaanisqatsi, is the reason for intervention, and that intervention is the Shaman. To restore balance in human life, even on an individual level, requires more than positive thinking. It requires the manipulation and resolution of negative energy, which may interfere with that life's harmonious conduct.

On a larger scale, Shamanism has the power to correct the course of human history by restoring the balance of the human soul. That means reconnecting the human being to its home (Creation). To do that, the energies that have thrown the organism out of balance must be rebalanced and renewed, bearing in mind the purpose of healing.

Shamanic Energy Healing

The wounds that live in all of us, no matter the event or events which caused them, are energetic realities. Unresolved trauma is emotional and spiritual scar tissue. These "soul adhesions" hold us in developmental stasis. We say that "some people never grow up," and that's sadly true. Trauma – soul adhesions – are the reason for that arrested development. We are held in suspended animation at the age when our most brutalizing trauma occurred.

As stated above, energy intrudes on the material when it's not appropriately balanced. In the instance of trauma, this intrusion can be life-altering, even life-destroying. Shamanic energy healing seeks to remove the energetic blockage of trauma to restore homeostasis by restoring the soul. This achieves balance in spirit, emotions, intellect, and the physical self.

Repairing and Retrieving the Soul

There are several indicators of energetic imbalance. These manifest until the balance is restored by energetic healing:

- Inappropriate beliefs about the self. This manifests as beliefs that undermine progress in life, happiness, and tranquility. Because "It's always been that way," you believe that it "will always be this way," allowing the trauma to dictate the quality of your life

- Health that's never robust; always less than optimal

- Patterns in your life and old stories you tell yourself to keep you from moving forward out of fear

- Mental health challenges, especially anxiety and depression

- The belief that you cannot break out of the toxic feedback loop you are in (energetic soul imprisonment provoked by low self-esteem).

When trauma is addressed with the help of Shamanic energy healing, you are repairing and retrieving your soul. This action affects all other aspects of the human organism you are – your physical health, your mental health, and your spiritual health. You return to balance, resulting in:

- Acceptance of life as it is, accompanied by the ability to keep going (another Hopi concept is to continue moving, regardless of adversity). The healed soul is resilient and unafraid

- The restoration of physical health, allowing the healing of long-standing, debilitating challenges

- The acknowledgment of your inner voice and the ability to heed its promptings, unconcerned with what others think and in complete trust

- The ability to understand your autonomy and personal power as a human being and to use them for your own good and that of your community

Clearing Existing Energy in the Physical Space

The Shaman works to retrieve the soul damaged by trauma by using Shamanic Journeying (which we'll cover shortly). But before that can be accomplished, the space itself must be cleared of existing energies to enable the ceremony to follow in a clean space. This Shamanic container is further fortified by creating the sacred circle (see Chapter Seven).

All spaces contain energies, for better or worse. Spaces used for ceremony hold energies for various reasons, energy from events that have occurred there, spiritual presences which have not been invited but have presumed to be present, and the vestigial energies of those who have passed through the space. These energies can be negative and must be cleared if soul adhesions are to be cleared there.

When intuition is given its proper place, energies become apparent. You'll feel the energies around you as either benevolent/positive or malevolent/negative. You'll sense energies that give rise to your intuition's opinion, at which point your reason will either confirm or negate the sensation. But when your intuition is in its proper place, the opinion you receive will always be accurate. The repaired, restored soul can sense accurately.

Deploying articles from Chapter Three (especially the drum, leaf, and other rattles, and the smudge stick), the space is cleared with the intention that has been fostered over several days, if not longer. The intention must be crystallized and then internalized for the clearing to proceed. Ask yourself why you're clearing the space. The answer is the intention, "To remove unwelcome energies from this space."

When prepared, the space should be approached as a living thing, with the Shaman prepared by intention to clear those energies that don't belong there. Do so compassionately, as some of the energies hanging around may be spirits with the trauma of their own. Acknowledge it and liberate them from lurking.

With intention, the tools you use matter much less. If you have *only a smudge*, use that. If *only a rattle*, use that. Immerse yourself in your intuitive superpower to discern existing energies and then clear them with loving energy that reminds them of your purpose and sends them on their way.

In the next chapter, we will discuss the Four Directions regarding ceremony and ritual and how to open the circle.

Chapter Seven: The Four Directions – Opening the Circle

The circle is an ancient representation of time, alluding to eternality in the form of a continuous, unbroken line that travels ever forward, continually departing and arriving at its starting point.

The circle is primordial. It's in the moon that hangs in the sky and its cycles. You could go as far as to contend that the full moon is the model for the Medicine Wheel and its circular temporal construct. Its reliable phases spoke to Early Humanity, telling it a story about the passage of time and its eternal nature, never beginning or ending. Creation, in this model, is achieved from existing matter formed by the Divine Hand. This serves only as an ordering of what's already there, a bit like the Biblical Creation narrative, which refers to a still, dark, watery world.

Today, modern connotations adhere to the moon, but we all know that we'll see that it was full at its appointed time, just as it always has been. We no longer live in a world that acknowledges time as an eternal circle. We chose time's arrow, relentlessly moving forward, excluding the markers of the natural world – an error that has cost us tremendously. For it is the circle that restores our relationship with time and all it governs in Creation. The circle is our first guide and our first means of measuring the passage of time, reified in the monthly return of the full moon.

The Sacred Circle is, in fact, the Shamanic Container we discussed in Chapter Three. Within this circle, the Shaman finds freedom and the energetic clarity required to pursue the Shamanic Journey to the Three distinct Worlds of the spirits (see Chapter Eight).

Preparing the Sacred Circle

Many world spiritual traditions employ some version of the Sacred Circle. Even Christianity has a labyrinth, walked in meditation. But this form of the circle is an adaptation governed by a construct of religion that denies its connection to the natural world, and so the circle in this tradition loses its original power. In Shamanism, the circle is central to the practice, evidenced by the guiding influence of the Medicine Wheel.

The primordial power of the full moon, translated to spiritual use by humanity for both its shape and ancient governance of time and tide, is at the heart of the Sacred Circle.

Having been cleared of all unwanted, negative energies, your ceremonial space is ready for the circle once your intuition tells you that the space is clean. This is something you'll have to trust me on; *your intuition can sense when the ritual space is clear.* Trust your intuition before you trust what has been written. It is your most reliable ally.

Before you begin, you need to establish the position of the Four Directions in your ceremonial space and mark them with a representation or symbol of either a plant, an animal, or a color to mark them and to guide your actions as you seek protection within the circle.

What Are You Protecting Yourself From?

The circle in Shamanism is used much the same as it is in other traditions relying on it. It protects the practitioner from the unseen energies threatening the safe and successful conduct of healing and discernment rituals, especially Shamanic Journeying.

If the Shaman is to be truly free to transition between worlds spiritually, then the absence of negative energies must be complete. That is why intention is so crucial in the clearing-circle casting-journeying complex of ritual activity. It is your intention that stands as both your power and your weakness. Because when you set an intention to heal, you bring forth energies in need of healing themselves, but this ritual is not for them. The clearing in which you have compassionately acknowledged the trauma of these energies was for them. The circle is not. So, that must be part of your intention in casting the Sacred Circle or Shamanic Container.

The spirit world may interpret your intention to heal as an invitation to draw nearer. But the presence of damaged spirits is an invitation to chaos. Those spirits are only concerned with their own damage, long since done during their earthly lives. They are no longer living, and their wounds, having been carried with them into the spirit world, can destroy the energetic purity of your circle, your ceremonial space, and the work you are doing.

Therefore, as you prepare to cast your circle, your intention should be abundantly clear – that only those energies united in the purpose of healing with the Shaman are invited to enter the circle, adding their presence and power to your own, to the benefit of the person who is being healed. Don't be afraid to be resolute in your intuition or to specifically deny entry to spirits you sense are coming forth to draw from you the healing they didn't know in life. You can only sympathize compassionately. You cannot heal the spirits of those already departed except via generational trauma healing, which is indirect through the descendent seeking healing.

Your work is with the living, so protect yourself from needy spirits. Be forthright and unwavering in ensuring that they are aware that they are in the wrong place and that they are not welcome. Know your power. Stand in it.

A Spiritual Container

The protective Sacred Circle safeguards the practice. Whether a Shaman has cast it or someone who is doing personal, spiritual work on their own behalf, this is the space in which the person the circle envelopes is safe and free.

The Four Directions are the starting point of the Sacred Circle. You may even wish to create a representation of a simple Medicine Wheel, with the associated colors painted into the four quadrants. The stable Directions and their attributes are your starting point for the Sacred Circle.

Choose a plant, animal, or both for each of the directions. If you're creating a Medicine Wheel, you'll be making the colors associated present in that representation. It is your circle. Call on the markers that appeal to you and to which you feel a kinship.

How you represent Bear, Eagle, Wolf, Buffalo, Cedar, Sage, Sweetgrass, and Tobacco is up to you. The simplest way, of course, is to employ the plants. If you live in an area that is not their natural home, they are readily available from various sources. But if you would rather use a drawing, a photograph, or a graphic image, these are perfectly acceptable. This is also true of animals. What is most important is how you acknowledge the Four Directions.

Elevating the Four Directions

Starting with the north, with your intention firmly set to invite only the energies most invested in earthly healing into the Sacred Circle to the exclusion of all others. Pray fervently, adapting the following example to the one you're comfortable with:

"Brother-Sister Bear, you recede in winter and renew in spring, emerging from the sleep of death to new life. With the scent of sweetgrass, you awaken to eternity in power. In your heart is the fire of eternity.

Brother-Sister Eagle, you soar in the freedom of the air, commanding the heavens. The scent of tobacco calls forth ancestors to celebrate the new life of the earth in its renewal. From you, we learn the freedom of eternity.

Brother-Sister Wolf, you are the seat of our instincts and the wisdom born of survival. The mighty cedar is your sheltering cousin. You teach us the wisdom of the earth as the guardian of our future selves.

Brother-Sister Buffalo, in your steadfast nurture, you sustain us just as the clear waters of the land do. Sage is your glory and your healing gift. You teach us that loving sacrifice is the true freedom of living.

Brother-Sister spirit animals, I pray you might grant me your medicine for the healing to be accomplished here today. With the humble presence of your virtues, the soul adhesions that bind us will today be healed."

Your smudge should be lit as you move around the Sacred Circle, honoring and elevating the Four Directions. As you pray, move the smoke from the smudge over the representations you have placed in the Directions. When you have prayed at all four sides, smudge yourself, again clearly transmitting intention and an invitation to friendly, helpful spirits.

When your ritual is complete, the circle will need to be humbly closed to signal the spirits that the work is accomplished.

Every time you intend to work in your ritual space, the circle must be created. This is to protect you for the reasons discussed above. But it is also for the sake of creating a container for your power and for that of the spiritual entities invited to participate in the work of healing. Within the Sacred Circle is power confined to a specific area. Like "canned heat," power is magnified in containment and condensed to become something formidable. And when the spirits join you in the circle, there is even more power.

The circle is dependent on your intuitive powers, the strength of intention you have created it with, and your ability to effectively cleanse the ceremonial space of unwanted energies. The words you say, the tools you use, and the appearance and articles in your space are more like visual aids than crucial aspects of the ceremony and the Sacred Circle you create there. What matters most is the purity of purpose and intention and the humility you bring to the ritual activity.

Wrapping Your Heart around the Journey

The next chapter in this book is probably the one of most interest to readers. We have all heard of Shamanic Journeying. To be clear, this is not an undertaking to be approached frivolously. This is not an Ouija Board. While your curiosity is to be commended, you are here to learn. But if you are here to read about this intensely spiritual and transcendent feature of Shamanism for the sake of personal amusement, one has to wonder why.

There is nothing "fun" about Shamanic Journeying. This practice is only attempted after serious preparation and diligent training. The Shaman must be tested in vocation and personal attributes and aptitudes to be considered a Shaman and, very often, only chosen for the role when born into a Shamanic lineage.

While you must understand that Modern Shamanism is a popular framework of exploration for the Western seeker, appropriating the role of Shaman for purposes other than those specified by shamanic traditions is arrogant and ill-considered.

As you read further, it is hoped and trusted that you'll read in the spirit of humility. Respect for the ancient practice of Shamanism, a global tradition that has endured for many thousands of years, over 100,000 according to some sources, is not only recommended, but it is also *imperative.* The act of journeying is pursued for specific purposes, serving the community of the living by connecting it with the wisdom of the ancestors and spirit guides. There is no room in this practice for people who think it's a lark or easy in any way.

Now that we've got that out of the way, it's time to move into the next chapter. This chapter on Shamanic Journeying is the reason we clear the space and the reason for the ceremony. The Shaman's journey is a journey of the soul beyond the veil. It's the breaching of time and space for the purpose of opening lines of communication to benefit the living and please the ancestors.

Prepare to read about one of the fascinating manifestations of human spirituality still living in our midst today.

Chapter Eight: Journeying to Non-Ordinary Reality

This is the chapter many readers have been waiting for. What you are about to read is a description of the preparations, tools, and actions required for Shamanic Journeying. We will also discuss the Shamanic Journey itself.

The first thing to say to you is that safety is your first concern. What Shamanic Journeying entails is a transition between worlds, which is no small matter. As stated at the conclusion of the previous chapter, this is not for *triflers*. So, expect this chapter to be quite involved and longer than those you have read in the rest of the book. This is a subject deserving of a thorough treatment and a careful approach, which we counsel anyone considering Shamanic Journeying to take. Part of taking care of yourself and your safety is not using any fire or open flame in the Sacred Circle.

But one of the most responsible things we can do is tell you not to attempt Shamanic Journeying of any kind until you have a genuinely thorough grounding of the practices involved. The use of ayahuasca and peyote are for trained and experienced Shamans, not for lay people. This book's title is not "A Course for Shamans." This is not Harry Potter. This is a book written for your interest and information, not to teach you "How to become a Shaman in just 10 days". That's not our purpose, and we hope that we have made that clear.

With all that said, we would ask that any attempt on your part to journey to the parallel worlds of non-ordinary reality be undertaken in humility and in the understanding that this book is an introduction to Shamanism and by no means to be viewed as a comprehensive "How to." we are not Shamans, and neither are you if you're reading this book.

Your humility and love are powerful and to be uplifted in any spiritual undertaking, especially one within an ancient framework that is not native to you. Learn deeply. Love deeply. Approach with humility.

Non-Ordinary Reality

As you read, you inhabit ordinary reality, the material world. Parallel to it is what we refer to as the "world of the spirits" or "the spirit world." But in Shamanism, this world is actually three distinct worlds.

While not universally present in all shamanisms, the "three worlds" cosmology is common enough among them to explore as a template. That template consists of the Upper World, the Middle World, and the Lower World.

Each of these worlds is unique and self-contained yet connected in the form of what is called "The World Tree" (see Chapter Two under Norse). This tree serves as a kind of axis, vertically connecting the worlds.

In the Upper World are the ascended ancestors and other Great Spirits we turn to when challenges arise. The Shaman journeys to this world to gain insight and knowledge, wisdom, and inspiration. The Upper World is the home of those whose journeys on earth and in the spirit worlds purified their souls.

You are now in the Middle World, inhabiting normative consciousness. But the Middle World has another layer, which is the layer of the spirits that reside in all that is. This spiritual aspect of the Middle World is unseen yet very present and parallel to our conscious waking reality. Shamans attend this world to commune with the spirits of nature and with Creation itself.

The Lower World is where animal, plant, and nature spirits reside and where the spirit guides reside. It is also the home of those who have passed. Typically, when we hear the word "lower" mentioned in spiritual matters, especially when talking about a non-material reality, we think of Hell.

And while it is true that not everyone in the Lower World is cuddly and adorable, it is not analogous to the Christian concept of Hell, the place of eternal fire. The Lower World is not reserved for those who were evil and capricious in life. The Lower World is where the human soul is challenged and tried. The recovery and repair of a human soul will often take Shamans to the Lower World to investigate sources and seek the support of spirit animals.

All three of the worlds we have just discussed are considered "non-ordinary reality" in Shamanism. With respect to the Middle World, non-ordinary reality lives right under our noses in the material world. Of course, this cosmology embraces animism, which is central to world Shamanism. And the Shaman enters non-ordinary reality, in all three worlds, to do the crucial work of healing. The Shaman climbs the World Tree to affect this feat, moving between the worlds at will. This is the same way spirits move between the worlds.

The Tree's roots extend to the Lower World, while the Middle World is the stable trunk. The Upper World is supported by the branches of the World Tree. So, the cosmological construct of non-ordinary reality is based on the presence of a tree which joins all its worlds together, facilitating spiritual communication and the free movement of spirits and Shamans.

The Shaman's Reasons for Visiting

Highly situational, the Shaman's reasons for visiting one world over another are entirely linked to specific intentions in any given circumstance. What guides the Shaman's decisions in this respect is knowledge of the world and the sort of shamanic support available in each in terms of spiritual guidance and knowledge. Shamans will also discern the way forward for the healing of a soul according to the specific circumstances of the acquired wound being treated.

Each world has specific advantages for the Shaman, discernable only via experiencing the worlds from the individual Shaman's perspective. There are some specificities in each of these worlds, but those are highly generalized. Where the rubber meets the road is in the intention built up by the Shaman and the location of the specific support being sought, whether ascended ancestor, spirit guide, or the soft, natural urgings of the spirits of Creation.

Spirit Animals – The Lower World

In the Lower World, Shamans seek out the helpful presence of spirit animals. The spirit animal is more than a guide or helper, though. The spirit animal is the template for the human being's potential. As we have seen with the animals present in the 4 quadrants of the Medicine Wheel, they display certain characteristics often sought after by animals of our race. Their qualities are desirable, and with their spiritual friendship, Shamans can both learn the ways of the animal and its spiritual content, as well as turn to any of these animals to assist in the restoration of human souls damaged by trauma.

There are many spirit animals inhabiting the Lower World. Some of these animals come to the Shaman fleetingly with a one-time message. Others are present intermittently. Still, others may stay with the Shaman for weeks, months, or years. Each has a very specific role to play in the Shaman's work, and each is highly individualized in that role of each individual Shaman.

Spirit animals are the soul analogs of their living counterparts in the Middle World, modeling their spiritual aspects, indicated in the observed behaviors and characteristics of the material animal. Like the human being and everything else in Creation, these creatures and their spiritual analogs are part of a greater reality in their species and in Creation, connected to all that is. We are all related, both materially and spiritually.

One distinguishing characteristic of the Lower World is its unitive purpose. In this world, there is no dividing line. There is only complete transcendence of speciation and separation. There are no rubrics to file creatures under in this world. It is a place of radical spiritual unity. The Lower World is the truth about the material world – that individualism is the enemy of spirituality. Because individualism is rooted in separation, it is not the reality of the Created Order, which is unity in diversity – a community that moves with a shared purpose in its diverse constituent parts.

The Role of Spirit Animals and Animal Guides

"One thing to remember is to talk to the animals. If you do, they will talk back to you. But if you don't talk to the animals, they won't talk back to you, then you won't understand, and when you don't understand, you will fear, and when you fear, you will destroy the animals, and if you destroy the animals, you will destroy yourself."

~ Chief Dan George

As pointed out above, spirit animals come to us with advice and counsel and reinforce the connected nature of Creation and its spiritual reality. They also come to remind us of their role in supporting the human goals of realized potential, in the traits for which they are known and admired. This is the "medicine" offered by the soul analogs in the Lower World.

The medicine of each animal is different, serving many healing projects by traits specific not only within species but within individual spirit guides and animals. They have stories, too, and those stories illuminate and drive the world of the Shaman. As Chief Dan George says above, "...talk to the animals.". They have much to share in the Lower World, and that sharing is constructive. It's also shared from the presumption of equality with the Shaman as a messenger from the material world. There is no hierarchy in the Lower World; there is only the transformative power of unity.

The work of spirit animals and animal guides is broadly defined under these categories, some of which we have touched on above:

- **Messenger**

  The messenger comes to impart a specific lesson or message, then leaves immediately

- **Shadow**

  The shadow is exactly what you might think it means. This is the guide that comes to us as our unresolved trauma/unhealed wounds. It comes to remind us that we have work to complete. This guide will come and go in various guises throughout life, according to the message being imparted

• **Lifetime**

This is your best buddy, accompanying you through a period of life to remind you of your strongest virtues and abilities and encouraging you to fully employ them for the greater good. A new teacher replaces this animal periodically, but there is always a "best buddy" spirit animal with you.

• **Journey**

When change is in the air and difficult, important decisions are being made. The journey guide will appear to advise you which way to turn at the fork in the road

• **Land**

Land animals come to offer stability and centeredness. When things are shaky, the appearance of a land-animal spirit guide means that you are going to get some help until stability is restored.

• **Water**

Animals who live in water bear freedom and purification. They are also intimately connected to the subconscious mind, revealing secrets from that mind's vault in dreams.

• **Bird**

Transformative change is signaled by the appearance of an airborne spirit animal/animal guide. With vision extending well beyond the horizon, airborne guides come to move you through obstacles to emerge transformed.

• **Reptile**

Reptiles adapt, so that's their message to you. They come to show you the silver lining, the way forward, and the intuitive solution to the problem you're grappling with. Remember, some of them shed their skins, so expect a snake if you're looking for a fresh start or a profound transformation, whether spiritual or physical.

- **Insect**

Insects survive. They persevere and work in the community. Should a global disaster occur, these guys are going to inherit the earth. Humble, tiny but enduring, insects are all about perseverance and survival.

As you have read, each of these categories serves a specific role and will appear according to intention, need, and purpose and the specific, applicable attributes of each of the categories described.

Every animal has a message to share with humanity. The spirit analogs model those attributes by spiritualizing them to work with the spirituality of human beings as our supportive guides and counselors.

Preparing for the Journey

The preparation for Shamanic Journeying is soberly conducted, with intention as the central reality of that preparation. Everything the Shaman does is rooted in a keen sense of mission in a specific interest, and that mission is translated into the intention.

Setting and internalizing intention is the single most important component of everything the Shaman does. In the instance of journeying, though, it's almost like a spiritual signal to the non-ordinary reality that a visit is imminent. The Shaman's well-formed and nurtured intention is heard as prior notice to the spirits that support is going to be sought. The intention further advises the nature of the support required, alerting spiritual entities concerned that they are on standby.

Setting Intention

The intention being the primary component of any Shamanic Journey, the Shaman's first job is to formulate a very specific one. Whatever the purpose of the projected journey, this intention is in the Shaman's mind from the moment they know that they are going to seek the support of the residents of the Three Worlds.

The intention is the Shaman's knowledge of the specific outcome desired. The Shaman will formulate intention with this outcome woven in. For example:

"I will journey to spirits of the Middle World to seek Nature's guidance concerning the health of my mother and return with the healing she requires."

The power is in the specificity. There is a clear statement of intention to journey to a specific world with a specific intention. As the Shaman repeats a clear, unequivocal intention like this, the spirit world listens and takes note. The intention is on the Shaman's lips and the mind, a heartbeat of intended action and outcome. It's all one thing because the Shaman's intuitive powers are well-developed.

Setting an intention is not unlike prayer. The mind and voice are lifted to send a request. This request is repeated in the spirit and physically propelled from the Shaman's lips in the form of speech, implicating the whole of their person. Tranquility is required to set an intention. Once set, the intention is internalized via continued repetition, making a purpose-driven home in the Shaman an active and living thing.

Your Conveyance – Sound

As pointed out in Chapter Five, few Shamans use mind-altering substances in the modern world, even in traditional frameworks. Latin America is where you're most likely to encounter Shamans using ayahuasca and peyote, of course, as these shamanistic allies are native to the Americas. But for the most part, this journey is made by riding the sound of the drum. Rattles may also be used and commonly are, but the drum is the heartbeat of humanity and its mission on earth. Its sound subconsciously reminds every ear that hears it of the sound of our mothers' heartbeats as we wait to join the living world.

In the sound of the drum is the story of humanity's existence, told through all its ages. Our ancestors heard it. We hear it. We feel it, and we respond to it by dancing, clapping, gathering, celebrating, praying, going to war, and going to the cemetery. The drum is our brother, joining us together in an unbroken line since the moment an implement was first taken up to strike an object, making a sound. From the moment we tied the skin of an animal to a section of a hollowed-out tree, the drum has been the heartbeat of our common Mother, the Earth.

On the sound of the drum, mellifluous and resonant, the Shaman rides, seeking the satisfaction of the presenting intention. The rhythmic soundscape achieved is the medium on which the Shaman rides. Slow and pulsating, this heartbeat is the guide to the state of consciousness that permits journeying.

Trance

The shamanic traditions of Central Asia and Siberia, the mother of all shamanisms, according to some, were some of the first to be analyzed by researchers from the Western World. It was here that the Shamanic trance was first observed.

The literal meaning of the word "trance" is "to cross over." From the Latin *transire*, the word describes the trance state as one in which a human being is enabled to move from the reality and consciousness they inhabit in daily life to another. And further, in that state of consciousness, they may encounter and interact with realities parallel to the one they normally inhabit.

At its root, the Shamanic Journey implicates the Shaman's spirit, intuition, and imagination, creatively weaving these human attributes together in a state of consciousness altered by the sound that drives their integration. That integration becomes a state in which trance occurs, and Shamanic Journeying may be provoked.

Pivotal to the achievement of a trance state is the will of the Shaman. The will to enter this state must be present. There can be no fear or doubt. There can only be the intention, framed as action and outcome. This state will occur when the Shaman is prepared by intention and willing to achieve the trance. When that's not the case, there will be no shift in consciousness.

So, if you're planning to attempt trance, ask yourself the right questions. Ask yourself if it is your will to enter a trance and to journey. Are you prepared mentally? Are you prepared for the spirit entities you'll encounter? Is your heart harboring fear or doubt? These questions must be responded to with total honesty. If your heart is not at the point of surrendering to the mission, you will not succeed.

The Journey

The Shamanic Journey, once launched, may not be interrupted. The trance state descends, and the journey commences, with the Shaman's intention driving his actions in the non-ordinary world.

The axis of the Three Worlds is the World Tree. On this axis, the Shaman (and spirits) move between the worlds to glean the information/healing/resolution being sought. The soul of the Shaman is released to travel to the parallel worlds, with a portion of its energies focused on the realms beyond and the task at hand: the retrieval and repair of the soul.

The Shaman may do this on behalf of another person or on their own behalf, seeking a solution to trauma that has damaged, fractured, or torn the soul apart. The Shaman's job is to encounter the spirit animals summoned by the transmission of focused intention, the ascended ancestors, or the spirits that dwell in Creation. Once in a trance, the Shaman will know who's who but only due to the strength of the intention that has been internalized and is now acting as a medium of communication with the spirit world.

The act of Shamanic Journeying is both spiritual and psychological. The traumas that root themselves in our bodies (of which the mind is an integral part and the command center of the whole) require a type of psychospiritual prognosis. The spirits themselves will provide guidance in this respect, but the act of journeying is, itself, part of the cure. It's in the journeying that the Shaman acts to resolve a psychospiritual problem, and that action is the "leap of faith" written by Soren Kierkegaard. We leap, not knowing. We leap, knowing. Shamanic Journeying is an act of extreme faith in the spirit world and the connection of awakened human beings to that world.

What the Shaman sees on the journey is often a replica of the material reality, somewhat altered by its parallel nature. What's verdant and green on earth is abundantly so in non-ordinary reality, speaking to the human soul of eternity and what it may look like. But the Shaman sees from a unique perspective, understanding that spiritual realities live in tension with material ones. In that tension is the aesthetic alteration of our world as a revelation of spiritual truths.

Mountains, valleys, trees, rocks, streams, and the spirits that inhabit them may appear, then disappear. There is no static reality in the Three Worlds. Non-ordinary reality is a soulscape, a world in which the spirits make a home and conform to the ethereal nature of life in the spirit.

But each Shaman's experience of these worlds is different. Some retain an awareness of the physical, material space they are journeying from. Some can hear. Others can't. Some can speak. Others can't. Sensory abilities may be different from one journey to the next. But what's truly important is that intention, pursued diligently and internalized, will determine the information/healing the Shaman has come to obtain. And the process of obtaining it has begun the moment that intention becomes part of the Shaman's internal truth – that they have come to heal.

The senses in play while journeying are less important than the Shaman's ability to heal. The outcome matters because healing is the Shaman's primary role. The Shaman's sense of non-ordinary reality can be deceptive and by no means determines the Shaman's abilities. Everyone encounters the journey differently. Everyone senses differently during the journey. But the only thing that matters is what the Shaman returns with.

Trust

Trust is at the heart of Shamanic Journeying. There is no analysis while in a trance. There is no critical thinking. The Shaman has entered a parallel reality that doesn't play by our material rules. Animals advise rocks counsel, water sings, valleys recite poetry. Rejecting these variances, in reality, negates the trust required to obtain the object of the journey in healing/information.

Shamanism is not about "knowing" as much as it is about the numinous and experiencing that unknown and unseen reality as part of us. Accepting that we're part of all that is allows trust to arise, shutting off the internal critical voice seeking to make sense of what may not be measured against the material. Non-ordinary reality has its own logic. It makes its own sense. The Shaman must know this intuitively, with no empirical basis. What is intuitively known is not tested by empiricism; it is just *known*. As this is not the world of empirical data or zeroes and ones, trust is the only position from which the human soul may fully experience the riches of the Three Worlds and the healing they bring to human lives.

.Shamanic Journeying is not a "pleasure trip." It's not amusement, and it's not for those interested in anything but the role it plays in people's lives. The help that can be obtained by forging connections in the land of the spirits is help humanity needs. We have reached a dark, ominous time in human history. Up is down. Wrong is right. Humanity is challenged by its own innovation. Shamanic Journeying offers another way of understanding ourselves. That understanding holds in it the seed of global healing for all people.

Chapter Nine: Healing the Future with the Ancestors

"The spirit of an ancestor has the capacity to see not only into the invisible spirit world, but also into this world, and it serves as our eyes on both sides."

Sobonfu Somé

Readers will know that Western society has a strange relationship with the dead and with death, in general. We fear death. We loathe death. We even kid ourselves that death can be magically avoided, with post-human philosophies that suggest our bodies are the reason we don't live forever, forgetting that the mind is part of the body. We hope, instead, for the Raymond Kurzweil solution to be disembodied and eternal spiritual machines.

In the West, we're not very good at coping with the idea that we won't always be here because we don't understand the nature of death. We think of death as the conclusion of life. And that is true, but only in the material sense. In the spiritual sense, we are still woven into the fabric as Creation is an integral part of it.

While today, many Christian churches refer to the funeral service as a "celebration of life," we see eternity in very different terms than shamanic cultures do. Our vision of eternity is tied to personal virtue and holiness. "The good" go to Heaven, reserved for believers in Christ, while "the bad" go to Hell, reserved for the evil and for non-believers.

This dualism is not well supported even within the doctrines of the various iterations of the Christian Faith. Eternity is not something that may be privatized according to the personality traits and accompanying actions of individual human beings. We are, all of us, a spiritual amalgam of good and evil. There is no person who is entirely evil and vice versa. We are shadows and light living in the same organism.

Where the West applies judgment, Shamanism applies wisdom, primarily that learned through the ages of humanity and held in the eternal wisdom of the ancestors. What they knew in life is magnified in death. It is added to as they journey through the spirit world, encountering others who have left the material plane and experiencing the truth of the parallel and very real non-ordinary reality in which they dwell. Unseen but known in their connections to us, revealed in prayer, contemplation, and journeying, our ancestors stand ready to support us with their wisdom if only we'll acknowledge their presence.

Because the ancestors long for us to recognize them as part of our lives. Just as older living generations guide and support, the generations who have passed desire involvement in our transitions and decisions. They have been there before. Every question on our tongues has been answered for them. Every thirst quenched. Every pain soothed. There is no more mystery in the spirit world, and the ancestors want us to know what they do.

While we can't hope to access every fiber of knowledge the ancestors hold, we can certainly receive the support we need by forming relationships through prayer, contemplation, reflection, and the process of journeying.

The Nightmares of Your Ancestors

Think of your family as a long thread in the fabric of Creation, stretching back to the moment at which all matter became animated by the Divine Will. That thread consists of fibers. Some of the fibers in the thread will not even be human but our evolutionary precursors, transforming and transitioning through time to become the animal we are today, the Homosapien. At the end of the thread is you, or, if you have them, your children. All those fibers have stories. They lived and died from the material, passing over to the spirit world, and as they did so at their appointed time, they left behind imprints of the traumas they suffered in life.

So, part of the mission of Shamanism is to repair the trauma of the past as it exists in the family today. The Residential Schools which once existed in Canada and the United States present a contemporary example of generational trauma played out in the public sphere. Remember, please, that the last of Canada's residential schools closed in 1996. That is, during the lifetime of most living adults. The fallout of these colonialist attempts to "kill the 'Indian' in the child" through aggressive cultural integration, using the schools to do it is brutal. These "industrial schools" sought to remove the languages of First Nations children, the cultural practices, and the way of living known by Canadian First Nations peoples for thousands of years.

Children were removed from their families to live in the schools. First Nations families often followed children to the school, pitching teepees at a distance in the hope of seeing the children. Many children did not survive the indoctrination of the schools, as we now know (see Resources section), from the mass graves recently unearthed in Canada and the United States. In Canada, the toll is estimated to be between 10,00o and 25,000. In the USA, the number is approximately 40,000.

Today, the First Peoples of both North American nations continue to struggle with this ignoble history and its impact on their communities. Trauma has a price that continues to be exacted in criminality, mental illness, and domestic violence. To accompany the enduring pain and trauma of the residential schools, the 60s Scoop (the forcible removal of children from First Nations' families for adoption into white families) further assailed the health of First Nations families and communities. The toll exacted continues to devastate Peoples across Canada, as the rootless languish in a culture *not their own*, long removed from their truths and their loved ones.

And in Canada, the resolution is sought on a spiritual level in the absence of a concerted effort on the part of the government to address the sins of the past.

Healing Ancestral Wounds

The wounds all human beings are burdened with are built on older wounds, the wounds of our ancestors. This ancestral burden is carried until it is broken by a spirituality connected to the health of the whole, both material and spiritual. Brokenness, as in the example of the residential schools, is generational. The wounds survive through generations, manifesting in dysfunctional ways.

Families that carry ancestral burdens of trauma face the challenge of compounded spiritual scar tissue that has adhered to healthy tissue. The pain is carried forward, added to, and exacerbated with each generation with no frame of reference for addressing it.

Shamanism is that frame of reference. In its ancient cosmology, it offers hope to those whose lives play out in the shadow of ancestral trauma by offering a means of addressing it through the work of the Shaman. But the Shaman's work always begins in the heart that seeks succor and the alleviation of pain. Facing our pain by admitting that it is there is the first step.

Our culture demonizes mental illness and seems to have even less patience for people bearing the burdens of the past. We're told to "pull ourselves together," to "live in the now," and to forgive others to lighten the load. But these suggested "solutions" are just lipstick on a pig when you're discussing generational trauma, borne in the living body as a fresh wound, perpetuated by fear and ignorance.

The pain felt by the children and grandchildren of residential school survivors is real. Cultures that had existed for thousands of years were destroyed. Lives were destroyed. Children died at the hands of a system that declared that who they were was not wanted. T that who they were needed improvement to please the colonial presence erected on land stolen from them. The pain of being hated as "lesser," "savage," "stupid," and "lazy" continues to live on in addiction, suicide, crime, and family breakdown in First Nations communities. But now, these same communities are reconnecting with the old ways cruelly ripped from their stewardship. Shamanism is healing generational trauma that has shamed two of the most admired nations on earth.

In July 2022, Pope Francis traveled to Canada to apologize for the Roman Catholic Church's role in the residential schools. This apology came in the wake of the discovery of thousands of children's graves on the grounds of these schools across Canada and the United States. This is also part of the healing that must be done in these communities, but the work must continue so that future generations may live free of generational trauma.

Reaching Out

Now that you have read a little about how to clear sacred space and how to protect yourselves within it, you are ready to set an intention concerning your ancestors. This action is a loving way to connect with those who have gone before you, to learn and grow spiritually. But it's also a deeply therapeutic journey you'll continue through your life if you're someone who's committed to understanding and humbly practicing a version of the shamanic traditions.

Your ancestors desire connection. They want you to know what you need to so that the ancestral trauma you carry in the cells of your body (see Chapter 10) may be healed. You may not heal so long as that trauma is actively living within you. Even those destined to become practicing Shamans of whatever tradition may be wounded but not by generational trauma. The adhesions of the ancestors can't be tugging at a living soul dedicated to healing others. The Wounded Healer carries a revelatory wound. The wounds of generations are not so much revelatory as millstones around our necks. A wound must speak of healing, not hellish generations of trauma. The full-throated entreaties of the past to be released in healing are not speech. They are red flags planted to draw our attention to truths that strangle our hope and our potential as human beings.

Reaching out to the ancestors draws you spiritually, mentally, and physically into your deepest self. In your cells, you carry the stories without knowing the whole truth about them. That truth is the switch that must be flipped for healing to begin. That truth is ugly and distorted and a reflection of the human organism in its fullness. We are darkness and light. We are evil and good. We know pain and pleasure. Trauma is an inevitable part of being alive, but trauma has no business outliving its moment through generations of needless suffering.

Set your intention as a prayer. Thank your ancestors for being present to you. Petition their wisdom and their words. Sit patiently to hear the story, and then thank them and praise them again for coming to your side to help you heal. They are healing in their way through your intervention, so it goes both ways. But with the ancestors, you are a mortal supplicant. Model the respect they deserve. Humble yourself to the ancient truths that they will share with you.

To guide you, this prayer can be reduced to a simple request to tell you whatever's on their minds when framed as an intention. Just remember that with every intention you develop for reaching out to the ancestors, obeisance is compulsory. These are the ancients you're communing with. You're bold to reach out, as few do. Just know your place and lead with a loving heart.

Ancestor Prayer

"I thank you and praise you, my beloved ancestors walking with me through time. I come to you to humbly solicit your wisdom and words. I ask that you share with me what you wish me to know to bring healing to the heart of our family. I thank you and praise you, beloved ancestors walking with me through time."

Wear white clothing to your sacred space, and once it's cleared in the manner discussed in Chapter 5, you can begin creating your protective circle, to which you'll be inviting the presence of the ancestors.

As stated earlier, this brief, forthright prayer is easily condensed into an intention that should be said for several days before you go to your ceremonial space. Keep it simple and strong, and roll it around in your head often. Internalize the intention into every fiber of your being to alert the ancestors of your plan to reach out. Say it out loud. Say it to your cat. Just hold it inwardly, circulating it through you to begin forging the spiritual connection with your ancestors.

The Joy of Working with the Ancestors

The mission of healing, shared with your ancestors as a family project, is a journey of joy. As you work together and you come to understand where you've really come from, you'll learn more about yourself through the connection forged with the ancestors than you ever thought possible.

The ancestors are all part of you. What you are is made of them. The stuff of their lives is active within you, and when that stuff is trauma – especially trauma that's rooted in ignorant hatred – you can't be entirely well. Your function is affected, and your wellness is suppressed. The ancestors know this better than anyone. And their investment is a long-term one. As much as they want their healing to take place, yours is the one that's most crucial, as it leads to theirs. In your healing is the healing of the future and the people that will come. Acting in the interests of the future is the joy of working with the ancestors, and their joy is in working with you to heal that future.

Societies that have actively suppressed or have unthinkingly abandoned the veneration of ancestors are largely those in which one of the three major monotheistic Faiths is dominant. Islam is one example of its suppression of the Sufi minority. Christianity is another discouraging ancestral veneration as a Pagan practice due to historical grudges that are now well over 2,000 years old. Despite several somewhat spurious attempts to attribute ancestral veneration to ancient Israel, Judaism features no such notable prohibitions, particularly when a violation of them is met with violence.

Venerating our ancestors is a means of understanding that we are people of great value, formed from generations of those who have come before. This is a high and spiritual concept of humanity that must return to us if we are to survive because all human beings have the same story. We are all long-term investments created from the epochs of humanity.

In knowing our ancestors, we come back to ourselves and our humanity. This alone is of tremendous value to all. But there is so much more ancestral veneration can achieve. When trauma has been healed in the loving embrace of the ancestors, life can realize its promise. The shadows cleared, and the way forward is defined, rising to meet you in your rebirth, freed from generational trauma and connected with your core truths. This is how the future is born – in the reduction of burdens that can hinder it.

In our final chapter, we will look at the promise of Shamanism and how it answers the reality of trauma as the driver of multiple human challenges. We can build hope in the world with the wisdom of Shamanism and that of our ancestors. We can build that hope by releasing the human mind and body from the trauma of past generations, as well as the contemporary trauma of the living.

The value to humanity of the Shamanic veneration of ancestors is immeasurable. It holds the key to the healing that must begin to restore humanity to health. We included the thoughts explored in Chapter 10 to be clear about the incredible value Shamanic cosmology, particularly with respect to the ancestors, holds out for this unhappy world.

Chapter Ten: Healing Humanity with Shamanism

Anyone who hasn't noticed how profoundly broken people are in our time isn't paying attention. This brokenness is endemic, appearing in places that look entirely normal, even perfect. But that perfection hides a truth that's unknown and yet forcefully present in almost all human lives to some degree – generational trauma.

There is no person living who does not harbor generational trauma. And, as I hinted at in the last chapter, that trauma is not experienced intellectually. How can it be when we don't know about the trauma? While we're talking about departed relatives from recent generations when we say "ancestors," we're also talking about people whose existences were never recorded because systems of writing hadn't yet been developed. They are your ancestors too, and of course, you have no idea what they went through.

Generational trauma is experienced in the body, existing at the cellular level (see Resources). Neurobiology has determined that the cost of trauma is physical, existing as an unknown hitchhiker in the bodies of the victims' descendants. While we are blissfully unaware of its unwelcome presence, when it's the generational variety transmitted through countless ancestors, it can be a problem.

Imagine a World without Trauma

As we have already said, trauma is inevitable. But why? Why do bad things happen not only to bad people or even good people but to everyone? Why is that the way things are? Every one of us can expect a major physical trauma at some point in our lives. There will be psychological trauma of varying degrees, also. We all get a piece. Some trauma (like accidents or surgery) is unavoidable.

Some of us, though, are traumatized in ways the rest of us are unfamiliar with. For every First Nations residential school, there are nations ruined by needless war, the destruction of entire peoples, and a litany of large-scale evils that boggle the human mind, even though the human mind conceived of these events.

The Canadian doctor Gabor Maté's work has prompted us to examine the role of trauma occurring in childhood as the root of many societal ills and mental health challenges. He posits that childhood trauma leads to a disconnection with the truth of the core self/personality.

Trauma absorbed in childhood leads to aberrant coping mechanisms like addiction, which has been a centerpiece of Maté's work, especially in the Downtown Eastside of Vancouver, Canada, an area rife with the evils of drugs and alcohol addiction.

In this world of trauma, we seek to treat addiction without addressing its root cause. We seek to medicate conditions like ADD and ADHD in the same way. This superficial approach is at the heart of a society spinning its wheels as lives fall into the abyss.

Dr. Maté's therapeutic philosophy is Compassionate Inquiry, which seeks to drill down into the psyche to the point at which the child is separated from themselves and their ability to interact normatively with the world. It seeks the origin story of the trauma that has stuck to people who suffer not only from addiction but from illnesses like autoimmune disorders and even cancer.

Dr. Gabor Mate's work is on the right track. Addiction is not a willful rejection of a functional life. It is an inappropriate response to traumatic pain experienced at the most vulnerable time of life – childhood. Society tends to dismiss addiction as a choice, but this is an uninformed, judgmental stance. We wouldn't say that people deserved cancer. We wouldn't say they deserved fibromyalgia or lupus, but all these conditions originate in trauma.

Compassionate Inquiry, a method that seeks to get to the heart of trauma and correct its corrosive influence, is not that different from Shamanic healing. Shamanic healing seeks to address trauma, whether contemporary or generational, in much the same way, knowing that the wounds of the past live on in the now.

The past is never over until we're willing to confront it, name it, and heal its wounds decisively.

The Cost of Childhood Trauma

While there are numerous studies attempting to pinpoint the monetary cost of childhood trauma, few are dedicated to pinpointing the ongoing human cost. Because childhood trauma doesn't end with the child affected, as that child grows, others are affected. Everyone the child comes in contact with is affected. The eventual children of the traumatized child are affected. Their spouse or partner is affected. Sometimes, there are also victims of that traumatized child, unwitting whipping posts for a pain that won't subside. And so, the cycle continues through another generation.

Everywhere you look, it seems, the walking wounded live out their trauma in socially corrosive ways. Even the January 6th event in the USA's capital can be seen as an offshoot of childhood trauma, with the aggrieved taking out their anger on the symbols and physical mechanisms of democracy. Criminality, family dysfunction, domestic violence, murder, mayhem, and shooting after shooting all point to unresolved childhood trauma.

In Canadian prisons, First Nations healers are now seeking to address the trauma of indigenous inmates with symbolic healing, providing a background education for people disconnected from their traditions. While these traditions have been revived in community settings, the "Urban Indian" often has no contact with the revival. These shamanic healers fill the educational gaps so that the person struggling with trauma can partake in their own cultural practices.

It's telling that while indigenous Canadians comprise only 5% of the population, they make up almost 27% of incarcerated people. And while there has not yet been a rigorous study undertaken to gauge the effect of First Nations' healers connecting with indigenous inmates, the elders are connecting with them, restoring their birthright to indigenous practices, which have existed for thousands of years.

This takes us back to the loss of the core personality implicated in childhood trauma. Traumatized children learn to "not be." They learn that when they "are," they are punished. So, they shut down. They become taciturn, sullen, and aggressive. Instead of being who they were born to be, they become someone else, a facsimile of the original. That facsimile is a façade, hiding the truth about the person within, disconnected from their wholeness and their reality.

The result of this disconnection isn't just the illnesses, criminality, and addictions that we have already mentioned. It is a strong possibility that the traumatized child is developing some of the most destructive personality disorders in existence, such as sociopathy and narcissism, or even the mental illness, psychopathy.

The Rise of "The Shadow"

The term "shadow self" was first coined by iconic psychoanalyst Carl Jung (1875-1961), describing the submerged parts of our personality, or the sublimated personality as a whole.

While those parts of our personality or our core personality aren't necessarily dark, our reasons for rejecting them most certainly are, especially in the case of childhood trauma. We reject our inner selves as the site of torment, not wishing to associate ourselves with it for fear the trauma will arise again. But to overcome trauma, we need to know the shadow and embrace it. When we fail to do this work, the shadow is still present, and it's present in dysfunctional, destructive ways.

In the three personality disorders named, the core personality is no longer active. It has been transformed, that is, sublimated or re-worked, to become "sublime" in the opinion of the person transforming it. This process is by no means conscious. It's a remedial process that takes place over time, as an alternative personality is being constructed to replace it. That alternative personality is, in fact, the shadow itself. Because of the systematic sublimation of the original personality, all the ills that are attached to it are now transferred to the new personality, presenting itself as the unruffled, unemotional, unempathetic, and merciless shadow.

While mileage varies on the presence of these personality types and psychopathy in society, their influence is clear. Adolf Hitler was a narcissist (formerly known as a "megalomaniac"), for example. Recent events in the world reveal that other leaders are similarly psychologically distorted. And when the shadow rules over a broken person, everything and everyone around them must be broken.

These three psychological disturbances account for untold harm, both in the micro and macro. And all three of them are rooted in the replacement of the original personality, with the shadow of trauma being resurrected as a new and noxious personality that wreaks havoc. There is no psychoanalytic approach proven effective for the treatment of narcissism, sociopathy, or psychopathy. But Shamanic healing has not yet been applied to this problem.

With its philosophical similarities to Gabor Maté's Compassionate Inquiry, I would argue that Shamanic healing is an answer that hasn't yet been tried or even considered. But as Shamanism continues to gain followers, it's possible that it may yet have an influence over treating what has been deemed "untreatable" by science and by society.

Shamanic Healing: Old Wounds a Specialty

Rage, envy, resentment, and hatred should never be the human legacy, yet as you read, much of what we see around us is characterized by these words and the emotional chaos that attends them.

Armed gangs attack their own government and fellow citizens. A madman, obsessed with power and expansionism, attacks another nation. People's rights are stripped from them, especially women. Sexual assault and armed attacks on schools, malls, churches, cinemas, and every other place people gather in the USA have become so common now that all we do is blink, offering "thoughts and prayers" until the next insult to human life occurs. Then, we blink again. We offer our impotent platitudes again.

We have become inured to the suffering we live next door to. We may even be inured to the suffering in our family, as many of us are rapidly losing our human ability to empathize and extend compassion to others.

In the practice of Shamanic healing and the general beliefs used in global Shamanism, there is an answer as old as time and yet, new to many of us. While we can't ignore the fact that some see Shamanism as a great way to make a buck, we'll assume that most practitioners have the best intentions. Those intentions, for those reading, should be clear if you've read closely through this book – to bring healing and wholeness to wounded people.

Individualism has not served us as a race. How could it, when humanity is a communal, social animal? We live more fully in the community. We live more supported, purposeful lives in the community. We are naturally adapted to this model of living. And at the heart of the community, when it's intentional and real, is healing. Mutual, loving support builds up broken hearts, making them stronger. That may only be had in the community.

We all walk this Earth wounded. Some are never healed. Some are healed only with intense introspection and time. Still, others seek the ancient knowledge of Shamanism. But the profile of this primordial way of being human is rising in the public consciousness, calling humanity toward it as a solution to its endless ills.

Reconnecting to the self is a spiritual pursuit. It takes us to frightening places we don't want to visit. But visit we must, climbing the World Tree from world to world to discover the riches that abide with the spirits of nature, the spirits of the deceased, and the spirits of those who have no name and may never have been human, to begin with. These parallel worlds are the home of lost wisdom which may only be recovered with the help of a skilled Shaman, the Wounded Healer.

The Wounded Healer is a guide to the heart and the core of who we were before we were broken. Many of us aren't even aware of the wounds we carry through life, but those wounds manifest in dysfunctional, often anti-social ways. We lean on the horn in traffic, knowing that everyone is in the same gridlocked boat. We jump the line at the grocery store, even though the person we've jumped in front of is 80, using a mobility scooter, and has only one item to purchase. We chew out the barista for betting the foam wrong on our cappuccino. Our wounds speak whether we want them to or not.

And so, it is in addressing our wounds that the healing of humanity may be accomplished, and in that, healing is another way of being human. It's a better way that's rooted in wholeness and radical honesty with the self. Instead of burying the shadow only to eventually wear it as a falsely constructed personality, we need to confront it. Instead of ignoring our wounds, we need to heal them. Where psychoanalysis has failed, primordial, shamanic healing has a place, offering great promise to a world in desperate need of healing.

Every Good Thing Was Once a Dream

Dreaming has a bad name for many. We consider it a waste of time or, even worse, willful indolence. But there's nothing lazy or wasteful about dreaming. Rather, dreaming is where every good thing starts.

Today, you are reading this book, hoping to derive more information about Shamanism. Tomorrow, you may study to become a Shaman. You may stay as you are, with some new knowledge that enriches your life. But in reading, you are seeking, and in seeking, you are dreaming.

Dr. Martin Luther King Jr. had a dream that changed the USA and the world beyond its borders. Nelson Mandela sat in a South African jail for 27 years to see his dream of dismantling apartheid (segregation) realized. Susan B. Anthony dreamed of a nation that rejected the enslavement of human beings and extended human rights to women, including the right to vote. Their dreams came true because they lived them in every fiber of their beings.

Your dream is one we're not familiar with, but if you've read through this book, it is hoped it will now include becoming more familiar with Shamanism and perhaps making space for it in your life. Everything good starts with a dream. If you dream of changing the world – even your small corner of it – the practice of Shamanism is one of humanity's most noble moments, enduring through time to bring healing to millions. Imagine that healing sweeping over the earth, healing the wounds of billions.

It's a dream. But it can come true, and you may be one of the reasons why.

Conclusion

Thank you for joining me on this journey into Shamanism and its potential to change the world in radically positive ways. Your interest in this subject gives me great hope that this change might happen. All change is a process. But the need is urgent, especially with respect to the health of the Creation, which is our home. We're part of this vast universe woven into it. The health of Creation is our health.

And as the planet groans with insults, our health diminishes. As discussed in the last chapter of Shamanism for Beginners, we're generally not doing well as a race. Eruptions of violence, displays of extreme entitlement, and the will to power hobble us now more than they ever have. The trauma we carry within us cries out for healing as we act out, damaging others and further compromising our own souls. Shamanic healing and its focus on ancestral trauma offer a path forward, providing a spiritual remedy that reconnects us with our sacred source and our value as human beings.

If you have read the brief introduction to Shamanism with interest, it is hoped you won't stop seeking it. Shamanism may not be your path. You may simply be interested in knowing more about it for your own edification. But if your interest in Shamanism is a personal one that you have been drawn to by signs, dreams, symbols, or by simple attraction, We hope and trust that you'll continue to explore it as a means of self-healing and for the healing of others.

Every day that passes, the need to heal Creation and its creatures grow more urgent. We need bold souls. We need Wounded Healers prepared to commit themselves to that project of global healing, one person, one plant, one animal, one river, lake, and ocean at a time. Passion and humility will lead us to the healing we seek, standing on the shoulders of countless generations of human healers living in spirit all over the world.

You have come to this book as a seeker after wholeness in primordial human spirituality. May what you've read spur you forward as a messenger of hope and healing, the bearer of old ways whose day now dawns again.

"The first lesson from our creator is to exercise respect,
for all creation comes from the spirit."

Shirley Bear

Here's another book by Silvia Hill that you might like

UNLOCKING SECRETS OF RUNE DIVINATION, NORDIC MAGIC AND PAGANISM, ASATRU, RITUALS, SPELLS, AND READING ELDER AND YOUNGER FUTHARK RUNES

SILVIA HILL

Free Bonus from Silvia Hill available for limited time

Hi Spirituality Lovers!

My name is Silvia Hill, and first off, I want to THANK YOU for reading my book.

Now you have a chance to join my exclusive spirituality email list so you can get the ebooks below for free as well as the potential to get more spirituality ebooks for free! Simply click the link below to join.

P.S. Remember that it's 100% free to join the list.

~~$27~~ FREE BONUSES

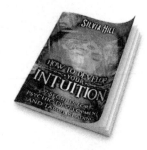

🖖 9 Types of Spirit Guides and How to Connect to Them

🖖 How to Develop Your Intuition: 7 Secrets for Psychic Development and Tarot Reading

🖖 Tarot Reading Secrets for Love, Career, and General Messages

Access your free bonuses here

https://livetolearn.lpages.co/shamanism-for-beginners-paperback/

Resources

11 signs you're called to be A shaman. (2017, October 1). Daily Informator. https://dailyinformator.com/11-signs-youre-called-to-be-a-shaman/

Are narcissists and sociopaths increasing? (n.d.). *Psychology Today.* https://www.psychologytoday.com/us/blog/5-types-people-who-can-ruin-your-life/201804/are-narcissists-and-sociopaths-increasing

Beware of impostors. (2008, January 18). Epic of King Gesar. https://buryatmongol.org/beware-of-impostors/

Bhattacharya, S. (2014, November 5). The lifelong cost of burying our traumatic experiences. *New Scientist (1971).* https://www.newscientist.com/article/mg22429941-200-the-lifelong-cost-of-burying-our-traumatic-experiences/

Cooper, A. (2022, June 5). *Canada's unmarked graves: How residential schools carried out "cultural genocide" against indigenous children.* CBS News. https://www.cbsnews.com/news/canada-residential-schools-unmarked-graves-indigenous-children-60-minutes-2022-06-05/

Dan. (2012, November 15). *Shamanism.* Norse Mythology for Smart People. https://norse-mythology.org/concepts/shamanism/

Gill, N. S. (2007, March 13). *Creation of the world in Norse mythology.* Learn Religions. https://www.learnreligions.com/creation-in-norse-mythology-117868

Gilmour. (2019, March 15). *Growing sage: Your guide to planting & growing a sage plant.* Gilmour. https://gilmour.com/growing-sage

Green, I. (2021, January 24). How can I find my Spirit Animal? *Trusted Psychic Mediums.* https://trustedpsychicmediums.com/spirit-animals/how-can-i-find-my-spirit-animal/

Hay, M. (2022, April 1). *How the rage for sage threatens native American traditions and recipes.* Atlas Obscura. https://www.atlasobscura.com/articles/white-sage

Kedia, S. (2020, March 22). *Spirit animal list.* TheMindFool – Perfect Medium for Self-Development & Mental Health. Explorer of Lifestyle Choices & Seeker of the Spiritual Journey; TheMindFool. https://themindfool.com/spirit-animal-list/

Koyaanisqatsi (1982) / watch free documentaries online. (1982, April 28).

Mcclellan, S. J. (n.d.). *Core Shamanism: Commonalities of shamanic practices.* Shamanicspring.com. http://shamanicspring.com/uploads/1/3/4/5/134555711/article_mcclellan_what_is_shamanism.pdf

Private Mentors. (n.d.). *The approach.* Compassionate Inquiry. https://compassionateinquiry.com/the-approach/

Simpkins, A. (2019, October 2). *Indigenous healing in federal corrections.* Cle.Bc.Ca; The Continuing Legal Education Society of BC. https://www.cle.bc.ca/indigenous-healing-in-federal-corrections/

Stobo, D. (2019, March 30). *You can become a "shaman" in a 60-minute online workshop—and that's a scary thing.* Well+Good. https://www.wellandgood.com/regulations-for-shamans/

Waldram, J. B. (1993). Aboriginal spirituality: symbolic healing in Canadian prisons. *Culture, Medicine and Psychiatry, 17*(3), 345–362. https://doi.org/10.1007/bf01380009

Wigington, P. (2009, July 7). *Make your own smudge sticks.* Learn Religions. https://www.learnreligions.com/make-your-own-smudge-sticks-2562199

Wilkinson, M. (2017). Mind, brain and body. Healing trauma: the way forward: Mind, brain and body. Healing trauma: the way forward. *The Journal of Analytical Psychology, 62*(4), 526–543. (N.d.).

Printed in Great Britain
by Amazon

45859203R00066